WHAT IS MAN?

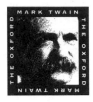

THE OXFORD MARK TWAIN

Shelley Fisher Fishkin, Editor

What
Is Man?

Mark Twain

FOREWORD

SHELLEY FISHER FISHKIN

INTRODUCTION

CHARLES JOHNSON

AFTERWORD

LINDA WAGNER-MARTIN

New York   Oxford

OXFORD UNIVERSITY PRESS

1996

OXFORD UNIVERSITY PRESS

Oxford   New York

Athens, Auckland, Bangkok, Bogotá, Bombay

Buenos Aires, Calcutta, Cape Town, Dar es Salaam

Delhi, Florence, Hong Kong, Istanbul, Karachi

Kuala Lumpur, Madras, Madrid, Melbourne

Mexico City, Nairobi, Paris, Singapore

Taipei, Tokyo, Toronto

and associated companies in

Berlin, Ibadan

Published by

Oxford University Press, Inc.

198 Madison Avenue, New York,

New York 10016

Library of Congress

Cataloging-in-Publication Data

Twain, Mark, 1835–1910.

What is man? / by Mark Twain; with an introduction
by Charles Johnson and an afterword by Linda
Wagner-Martin.

p. cm. — (The Oxford Mark Twain)

A facsimile reprint of the 1st ed. of Twain's work
including the original illustrations.

Includes bibliographical references.

1. Mind and body. 2. Philosophy of mind. 3. Man.
4. Philosophical anthropology. I. Title. II. Series:
Twain, Mark, 1835–1910. Works. 1996.

BF161.T93 1996

128—dc20

96-14729

CIP

ISBN 0-19-510154-5 (trade ed.)

ISBN 0-19-511421-3 (lib. ed.)

ISBN 0-19-509088-8 (trade ed. set)

ISBN 0-19-511345-4 (lib. ed. set)

9 8 7 6 5 4 3 2 1

Printed in the United States of America

on acid-free paper

FRONTISPIECE

This pensive view of Samuel L. Clemens was taken
by Vander Weyde of New York in 1906, the year
Clemens anonymously published *What Is Man?*
(The Mark Twain House, Hartford, Connecticut)

CONTENTS

EDITOR'S NOTE

The Oxford Mark Twain consists of twenty-nine volumes of facsimiles of the first American editions of Mark Twain's works, with an editor's foreword, new introductions, afterwords, notes on the texts, and essays on the illustrations in volumes with artwork. The facsimiles have been reproduced from the originals unaltered, except that blank pages in the front and back of the books have been omitted, and any seriously damaged or missing pages have been replaced by pages from other first editions (as indicated in the notes on the texts).

In the foreword, introduction, afterword, and essays on the illustrations, the titles of Mark Twain's works have been capitalized according to modern conventions, as have the names of characters (except where otherwise indicated). In the case of discrepancies between the title of a short story, essay, or sketch as it appears in the original table of contents and as it appears on its own title page, the title page has been followed. The parenthetical numbers in the introduction, afterwords, and illustration essays are page references to the facsimiles.

FOREWORD

Shelley Fisher Fishkin

amuel Clemens entered the world and left it with Halley's Comet, little dreaming that generations hence Halley's Comet would be less famous than Mark Twain. He has been called the American Cervantes, our Homer, our Tolstoy, our Shakespeare, our Rabelais. Ernest Hemingway maintained that "all modern American literature comes from one book by Mark Twain called *Huckleberry Finn.*" President Franklin Delano Roosevelt got the phrase "New Deal" from *A Connecticut Yankee in King Arthur's Court.* *The Gilded Age* gave an entire era its name. "The future historian of America," wrote George Bernard Shaw to Samuel Clemens, "will find your works as indispensable to him as a French historian finds the political tracts of Voltaire."[1]

There is a Mark Twain Bank in St. Louis, a Mark Twain Diner in Jackson Heights, New York, a Mark Twain Smoke Shop in Lakeland, Florida. There are Mark Twain Elementary Schools in Albuquerque, Dayton, Seattle, and Sioux Falls. Mark Twain's image peers at us from advertisements for Bass Ale (his drink of choice was Scotch), for a gas company in Tennessee, a hotel in the nation's capital, a cemetery in California.

Ubiquitous though his name and image may be, Mark Twain is in no danger of becoming a petrified icon. On the contrary: Mark Twain lives. *Huckleberry Finn* is "the most taught novel, most taught long work, and most taught piece of American literature" in American schools from junior high to the graduate level.[2] Hundreds of Twain impersonators appear in theaters, trade shows, and shopping centers in every region of the country.[3] Scholars publish hundreds of articles as well as books about Twain every year, and he is the subject of daily exchanges on the Internet. A journalist somewhere in the world finds a reason to quote Twain just about every day. Television series such as *Bonanza, Star Trek: The Next Generation*, and *Cheers* broadcast episodes that feature Mark Twain as a character. Hollywood screenwriters regularly produce movies inspired by his works, and writers of mysteries and science fiction continue to weave him into their plots.[4]

A century after the American Revolution sent shock waves throughout Europe, it took Mark Twain to explain to Europeans and to his countrymen alike what that revolution had wrought. He probed the significance of this new land and its new citizens, and identified what it was in the Old World that America abolished and rejected. The founding fathers had thought through the political dimensions of making a new society; Mark Twain took on the challenge of interpreting the social and cultural life of the United States for those outside its borders as well as for those who were living the changes he discerned.

Americans may have constructed a new society in the eighteenth century, but they articulated what they had done in voices that were largely inter-changeable with those of Englishmen until well into the nineteenth century. Mark Twain became the voice of the new land, the leading translator of what and who the "American" was — and, to a large extent, is. Frances Trollope's *Domestic Manners of the Americans,* a best-seller in England, Hector St. John de Crèvecoeur's *Letters from an American Farmer,* and Tocqueville's *Democracy in America* all tried to explain America to Europeans. But Twain did more than that: he allowed European readers to *experience* this strange "new world." And he gave his countrymen the tools to do two things they had not quite had the confidence to do before. He helped them stand before the cultural icons of the Old World unembarrassed, unashamed of America's lack of palaces and shrines, proud of its brash practicality and bold inventiveness, unafraid to reject European models of "civilization" as tainted or corrupt. And he also helped them recognize their own insularity, boorishness, arrogance, or ignorance, and laugh at it — the first step toward transcending it and becoming more "civilized," in the best European sense of the word.

Twain often strikes us as more a creature of our time than of his. He appreciated the importance and the complexity of mass tourism and public relations, fields that would come into their own in the twentieth century but were only fledgling enterprises in the nineteenth. He explored the liberating potential of humor and the dynamics of friendship, parenting, and marriage. He narrowed the gap between "popular" and "high" culture, and he meditated on the enigmas of personal and national identity. Indeed, it would be difficult to find an issue on the horizon today that Twain did not touch on somewhere in his work. Heredity versus environment? Animal rights? The boundaries of gender? The place of black voices in the cultural heritage of the United States? Twain was there.

With startling prescience and characteristic grace and wit, he zeroed in on many of the key challenges — political, social, and technological — that would face his country and the world for the next hundred years: the challenge of race relations in a society founded on both chattel slavery and ideals of equality, and the intractable problem of racism in American life; the potential of new technologies to transform our lives in ways that can be both exhilarating and terrifying — as well as unpredictable; the problem of imperialism and the difficulties entailed in getting rid of it. But he never lost sight of the most basic challenge of all: each man or woman's struggle for integrity in the face of the seductions of power, status, and material things.

Mark Twain's unerring sense of the right word and not its second cousin taught people to pay attention when he spoke, in person or in print. He said things that were smart and things that were wise, and he said them incomparably well. He defined the rhythms of our prose and the contours of our moral map. He saw our best and our worst, our extravagant promise and our stunning failures, our comic foibles and our tragic flaws. Throughout the world he is viewed as the most distinctively American of American authors — and as one of the most universal. He is assigned in classrooms in Naples, Riyadh, Belfast, and Beijing, and has been a major influence on twentieth-century writers from Argentina to Nigeria to Japan. The Oxford Mark Twain celebrates the versatility and vitality of this remarkable writer.

The Oxford Mark Twain reproduces the first American editions of Mark Twain's books published during his lifetime.[5] By encountering Twain's works in their original format — typography, layout, order of contents, and illustrations — readers today can come a few steps closer to the literary artifacts that entranced and excited readers when the books first appeared. Twain approved of and to a greater or lesser degree supervised the publication of all of this material.[6] The Mark Twain House in Hartford, Connecticut, generously loaned us its originals.[7] When more than one copy of a first American edition was available, Robert H. Hirst, general editor of the Mark Twain Project, in cooperation with Marianne Curling, curator of the Mark Twain House (and Jeffrey Kaimowitz, head of Rare Books for the Watkinson Library of Trinity College, Hartford, where the Mark Twain House collection is kept), guided our decision about which one to use.[8] As a set, the volumes also contain more than eighty essays commissioned especially for The Oxford Mark Twain, in which distinguished contributors reassess Twain's achievement as a writer and his place in the cultural conversation that he did so much to shape.

Each volume of The Oxford Mark Twain is introduced by a leading American, Canadian, or British writer who responds to Twain — often in a very personal way — as a fellow writer. Novelists, journalists, humorists, columnists, fabulists, poets, playwrights — these writers tell us what Twain taught them and what in his work continues to speak to them. Reading Twain's books, both famous and obscure, they reflect on the genesis of his art and the characteristics of his style, the themes he illuminated, and the aesthetic strategies he pioneered. Individually and collectively their contributions testify to the place Mark Twain holds in the hearts of readers of all kinds and temperaments.

Scholars whose work has shaped our view of Twain in the academy today have written afterwords to each volume, with suggestions for further reading. Their essays give us a sense of what was going on in Twain's life when he wrote the book at hand, and of how that book fits into his career. They explore how each book reflects and refracts contemporary events, and they show Twain responding to literary and social currents of the day, variously accepting, amplifying, modifying, and challenging prevailing paradigms. Sometimes they argue that works previously dismissed as quirky or eccentric departures actually address themes at the heart of Twain's work from the start. And as they bring new perspectives to Twain's composition strategies in familiar texts, several scholars see experiments in form where others saw only formlessness, method where prior critics saw only madness. In addition to elucidating the work's historical and cultural context, the afterwords provide an overview of responses to each book from its first appearance to the present.

Most of Mark Twain's books involved more than Mark Twain's words: unique illustrations. The parodic visual send-ups of "high culture" that Twain himself drew for *A Tramp Abroad*, the sketch of financial manipulator Jay Gould as a greedy and sadistic "Slave Driver" in *A Connecticut Yankee in King Arthur's Court*, and the memorable drawings of Eve in *Eve's Diary* all helped Twain's books to be sold, read, discussed, and preserved. In their essays for each volume that contains artwork, Beverly R. David and Ray Sapirstein highlight the significance of the sketches, engravings, and photographs in the first American editions of Mark Twain's works, and tell us what is known about the public response to them.

The Oxford Mark Twain invites us to read some relatively neglected works by Twain in the company of some of the most engaging literary figures of our time. Roy Blount Jr., for example, riffs in a deliciously Twain-like manner on "An Item Which the Editor Himself Could Not Understand," which may well rank as one of the least-known pieces Twain ever published. Bobbie Ann Mason celebrates the "mad energy" of Twain's most obscure comic novel, *The American Claimant*, in which the humor "hurtles beyond tall tale into simon-pure absurdity."[9] Garry Wills finds that *Christian Science* "gets us very close to the heart of American culture." Lee Smith reads "Political Economy" as a sharp and funny essay on language. Walter Mosley sees "The Stolen White Elephant," a story "reduced to a series of ridiculous telegrams related by an untrustworthy narrator caught up in an adventure that is as impossible as it is ludicrous," as a stunningly compact and economical satire of a world we still recognize as our own. Anne Bernays returns to "The Private History of a Campaign That Failed" and finds "an antiwar manifesto that is also confession, dramatic monologue, a plea for understanding and absolution, and a romp that gradually turns into atrocity even as we watch." After revisiting Captain Stormfield's heaven, Frederik Pohl finds that there "is no imaginable place more pleasant to spend eternity." Indeed, Pohl writes, "one would almost be willing to die to enter it."

While less familiar works receive fresh attention in The Oxford Mark Twain, new light is cast on the best-known works as well. Judith Martin ("Miss Manners") points out that it is by reading a court etiquette book that Twain's pauper learns how to behave as a proper prince. As important as etiquette may be in the palace, Martin notes, it is even more important in the slums.

> That etiquette is a sorer point with the ruffians in the street than with the proud dignitaries of the prince's court may surprise some readers. As in our own streets, etiquette is always a more volatile subject among those who cannot count on being treated with respect than among those who have the power to command deference.

And taking a fresh look at *Adventures of Huckleberry Finn,* Toni Morrison writes,

> much of the novel's genius lies in its quiescence, the silences that pervade it and give it a porous quality that is by turns brooding and soothing. It lies in . . . the subdued images in which the repetition of a simple word, such as "lonesome," tolls like an evening bell; the moments when nothing is said, when scenes and incidents swell the heart unbearably precisely because unarticulated, and force an act of imagination almost against the will.

Engaging Mark Twain as one writer to another, several contributors to The Oxford Mark Twain offer new insights into the processes by which his books came to be. Russell Banks, for example, reads *A Tramp Abroad* as "an important revision of Twain's incomplete first draft of *Huckleberry Finn,* a second draft, if you will, which in turn made possible the third and final draft." Erica Jong suggests that *1601,* a freewheeling parody of Elizabethan manners and mores, written during the same summer Twain began *Huckleberry Finn*, served as "a warm-up for his creative process" and "primed the pump for other sorts of freedom of expression." And Justin Kaplan suggests that "one of the transcendent figures standing behind and shaping" *Joan of Arc* was Ulysses S. Grant, whose memoirs Twain had recently published, and who, like Joan, had risen unpredictably "from humble and obscure origins" to become a "military genius" endowed with "the gift of command, a natural eloquence, and an equally natural reserve."

As a number of contributors note, Twain was a man ahead of his times. *The Gilded Age* was the first "Washington novel," Ward Just tells us, because "Twain was the first to see the possibilities that had eluded so many others." Commenting on *The Tragedy of Pudd'nhead Wilson*, Sherley Anne Williams observes that "Twain's argument about the power of environment in shaping character runs directly counter to prevailing sentiment where the negro was concerned." Twain's fictional technology, wildly fanciful by the standards of his day, predicts developments we take for granted in ours. DNA cloning, fax machines, and photocopiers are all prefigured, Bobbie Ann Mason tells us, in *The American Claimant*. Cynthia Ozick points out that the "telelectrophonoscope" we meet in "From the 'London Times' of 1904" is suspiciously like what we know as "television." And Malcolm Bradbury suggests that in the "phrenophones" of "Mental Telegraphy" "the Internet was born."

Twain turns out to have been remarkably prescient about political affairs as well. Kurt Vonnegut sees in *A Connecticut Yankee* a chilling foreshadowing (or perhaps a projection from the Civil War) of "all the high-tech atrocities which followed, and which follow still." Cynthia Ozick suggests that "The Man That Corrupted Hadleyburg," along with some of the other pieces collected under that title — many of them written when Twain lived in a Vienna ruled by Karl Lueger, a demagogue Adolf Hitler would later idolize — shoot up moral flares that shed an eerie light on the insidious corruption, prejudice, and hatred that reached bitter fruition under the Third Reich. And Twain's portrait in this book of "the dissolving Austria-Hungary of the 1890s," in Ozick's view, presages not only the Sarajevo that would erupt in 1914 but also "the disintegrated components of the former Yugoslavia" and "the *fin-de-siècle* Sarajevo of our own moment."

Despite their admiration for Twain's ambitious reach and scope, contributors to The Oxford Mark Twain also recognize his limitations. Mordecai Richler, for example, thinks that "the early pages of *Innocents Abroad* suffer from being a tad broad, proffering more burlesque than inspired satire," perhaps because Twain was "trying too hard for knee-slappers." Charles Johnson notes that the Young Man in Twain's philosophical dialogue about free will and determinism (*What Is Man?*) "caves in far too soon," failing to challenge what through late-twentieth-century eyes looks like "pseudoscience" and suspect essentialism in the Old Man's arguments.

Some contributors revisit their first encounters with Twain's works, recalling what surprised or intrigued them. When David Bradley came across "Fenimore Cooper's Literary Offences" in his college library, he "did not at first realize that Twain was being his usual ironic self with all this business about the 'nineteen rules governing literary art in the domain of romantic fiction,' but by the time I figured out there was no such list outside Twain's own head, I had decided that the rules made *sense*. . . . It seemed to me they were a pretty good blueprint for writing — Negro writing included." Sherley Anne Williams remembers that part of what attracted her to *Pudd'nhead Wilson* when she first read it thirty years ago was "that Twain, writing at the end of the nineteenth century, could imagine negroes as characters, albeit white ones, who actually thought for and of themselves, whose actions were the product of their thinking rather than the spontaneous ephemera of physical instincts that stereotype assigned to blacks." Frederik Pohl recalls his first reading of *Huckleberry Finn* as "a watershed event" in his life, the first book he read as a child in which "bad people" ceased to exercise a monopoly on doing "bad things." In *Huckleberry Finn* "some seriously bad things — things like the possession and mistreatment of black slaves, like stealing and lying, even like killing other people in duels — were quite often done by people who not only thought of themselves as exemplarily moral but, by any other standards I knew how to apply, actually *were* admirable citizens." The world that

Tom and Huck lived in, Pohl writes, "was filled with complexities and contradictions," and resembled "the world I appeared to be living in myself."

Other contributors explore their more recent encounters with Twain, explaining why they have revised their initial responses to his work. For Toni Morrison, parts of *Huckleberry Finn* that she "once took to be deliberate evasions, stumbles even, or a writer's impatience with his or her material," now strike her "as otherwise: as entrances, crevices, gaps, seductive invitations flashing the possibility of meaning. Unarticulated eddies that encourage diving into the novel's undertow — the real place where writer captures reader." One such "eddy" is the imprisonment of Jim on the Phelps farm. Instead of dismissing this portion of the book as authorial bungling, as she once did, Morrison now reads it as Twain's commentary on the 1880s, a period that "saw the collapse of civil rights for blacks," a time when "the nation, as well as Tom Sawyer, was deferring Jim's freedom in agonizing play." Morrison believes that Americans in the 1880s were attempting "to bury the combustible issues Twain raised in his novel," and that those who try to kick Huck Finn out of school in the 1990s are doing the same: "The cyclical attempts to remove the novel from classrooms extend Jim's captivity on into each generation of readers."

Although imitation-Hemingway and imitation-Faulkner writing contests draw hundreds of entries annually, no one has ever tried to mount a faux-Twain competition. Why? Perhaps because Mark Twain's voice is too much a part of who we are and how we speak even today. Roy Blount Jr. suggests that it is impossible, "at least for an American writer, to parody Mark Twain. It would be like doing an impression of your father or mother: he or she is already there in your voice."

Twain's style is examined and celebrated in The Oxford Mark Twain by fellow writers who themselves have struggled with the nuances of words, the structure of sentences, the subtleties of point of view, and the trickiness of opening lines. Bobbie Ann Mason observes, for example, that "Twain loved the sound of words and he knew how to string them by sound, like different shades of one color: 'The earl's barbaric eye,' 'the Usurping Earl,' 'a double-dyed humbug.'" Twain "relied on the punch of plain words" to show writers how to move beyond the "wordy romantic rubbish" so prevalent in nineteenth-century fiction, Mason says; he "was one of the first writers in America to deflower literary language." Lee Smith believes that "American writers have benefited as much from the way Mark Twain opened up the possibilities of first-person narration as we have from his use of vernacular language." (She feels that "the ghost of Mark Twain was hovering someplace in the background" when she decided to write her novel *Oral History* from the standpoint of multiple first-person narrators.) Frederick Busch maintains that "A Dog's Tale" "boasts one of the great opening sentences" of all time: "My father was a St. Bernard, my mother was a collie, but I am a Presbyterian." And Ursula Le Guin marvels at the ingenuity of the following sentence that she encounters in *Extracts from Adam's Diary*.

> . . . This made her sorry for the creatures which live in there, which she calls fish, for she continues to fasten names on to things that don't need them and don't come when they are called by them, which is a matter of no consequence to her, as she is such a numskull anyway; so she got a lot of them out and brought them in last night and put them in my bed to keep warm, but I have noticed them now and then all day, and I don't see that they are any happier there than they were before, only quieter.[10]

Le Guin responds,

> Now, that is a pure Mark-Twain-tour-de-force sentence, covering an immense amount of territory in an effortless, aimless ramble that seems to be heading nowhere in particular and ends up with breathtaking accuracy at the gold mine. Any sensible child would find that funny, perhaps not following all its divagations but delighted by the swing of it, by the word "numskull," by the idea of putting fish in the bed; and as that child grew older and reread it, its reward would only grow; and if that grown-up child had to write an essay on the piece and therefore earnestly studied and pored over this sentence, she would end up in unmitigated admiration of its vocabulary, syntax, pacing, sense, and rhythm, above all the beautiful

timing of the last two words; and she would, and she does, still find it funny.

The fish surface again in a passage that Gore Vidal calls to our attention, from *Following the Equator*: "'The Whites always mean well when they take human fish out of the ocean and try to make them dry and warm and happy and comfortable in a chicken coop,' which is how, through civilization, they did away with many of the original inhabitants. Lack of empathy is a principal theme in Twain's meditations on race and empire."

Indeed, empathy — and its lack — is a principal theme in virtually all of Twain's work, as contributors frequently note. Nat Hentoff quotes the following thoughts from Huck in *Tom Sawyer Abroad*:

> I see a bird setting on a dead limb of a high tree, singing with its head tilted back and its mouth open, and before I thought I fired, and his song stopped and he fell straight down from the limb, all limp like a rag, and I run and picked him up and he was dead, and his body was warm in my hand, and his head rolled about this way and that, like his neck was broke, and there was a little white skin over his eyes, and one little drop of blood on the side of his head; and laws! I could n't see nothing more for the tears; and I hain't never murdered no creature since that war n't doing me no harm, and I ain't going to.[11]

"The Humane Society," Hentoff writes, "has yet to say anything as powerful — and lasting."

Readers of The Oxford Mark Twain will have the pleasure of revisiting Twain's Mississippi landmarks alongside Willie Morris, whose own lower Mississippi Valley boyhood gives him a special sense of connection to Twain. Morris knows firsthand the mosquitoes described in *Life on the Mississippi* — so colossal that "two of them could whip a dog" and "four of them could hold a man down"; in Morris's own hometown they were so large during the flood season that "local wags said they wore wristwatches." Morris's Yazoo City and Twain's Hannibal shared a "rough-hewn democracy . . . complicated by all the visible textures of caste and class, . . . harmless boyhood fun and mischief right along with . . . rank hypocrisies, churchgoing sanctimonies, racial hatred, entrenched and unrepentant greed."

For the West of Mark Twain's *Roughing It*, readers will have George Plimpton as their guide. "What a group these newspapermen were!" Plimpton writes about Twain and his friends Dan De Quille and Joe Goodman in Virginia City, Nevada. "Their roisterous carryings-on bring to mind the kind of frat-house enthusiasm one associates with college humor magazines like the *Harvard Lampoon*." Malcolm Bradbury examines Twain as "a living example of what made the American so different from the European." And Hal Holbrook, who has interpreted Mark Twain on stage for some forty years, describes how Twain "played" during the civil rights movement, during the Vietnam War, during the Gulf War, and in Prague on the eve of the demise of Communism.

Why do we continue to read Mark Twain? What draws us to him? His wit? His compassion? His humor? His bravura? His humility? His understanding of who and what we are in those parts of our being that we rarely open to view? Our sense that he knows we can do better than we do? Our sense that he knows we can't? E. L. Doctorow tells us that children are attracted to *Tom Sawyer* because in this book "the young reader confirms his own hope that no matter how troubled his relations with his elders may be, beneath all their disapproval is their underlying love for him, constant and steadfast." Readers in general, Arthur Miller writes, value Twain's "insights into America's always uncertain moral life and its shifting but everlasting hypocrisies"; we appreciate the fact that he "is not using his alienation from the public illusions of his hour in order to reject the country implicitly as though he could live without it, but manifestly in order to correct it." Perhaps we keep reading Mark Twain because, in Miller's words, he "wrote much more like a father than a son. He doesn't seem to be sitting in class taunting the teacher but standing at the head of it challenging his students to acknowledge their own humanity, that is, their immemorial attraction to the untrue."

Mark Twain entered the public eye at a time when many of his countrymen considered "American culture" an oxymoron; he died four years before a world conflagration that would lead many to question whether the contradiction in terms was not "European civilization" instead. In between he worked in journalism, printing, steamboating, mining, lecturing, publishing, and editing, in virtually every region of the country. He tried his hand at humorous sketches, social satire, historical novels, children's books, poetry, drama, science fiction, mysteries, romance, philosophy, travelogue, memoir, polemic, and several genres no one had ever seen before or has ever seen since. He invented a self-pasting scrapbook, a history game, a vest strap, and a gizmo for keeping bed sheets tucked in; he invested in machines and processes designed to revolutionize typesetting and engraving, and in a food supplement called "Plasmon." Along the way he cheerfully impersonated himself and prior versions of himself for doting publics on five continents while playing out a charming rags-to-riches story followed by a devastating riches-to-rags story followed by yet another great American comeback. He had a long-running real-life engagement in a sumptuous comedy of manners, and then in a real-life tragedy not of his own design: during the last fourteen years of his life almost everyone he ever loved was taken from him by disease and death.

Mark Twain has indelibly shaped our views of who and what the United States is as a nation and of who and what we might become. He understood the nostalgia for a "simpler" past that increased as that past receded — and he saw through the nostalgia to a past that was just as complex as the present. He recognized better than we did ourselves our potential for greatness and our potential for disaster. His fictions brilliantly illuminated the world in which he lived, changing it — and us — in the process. He knew that our feet often danced to tunes that had somehow remained beyond our hearing; with perfect pitch he played them back to us.

My mother read *Tom Sawyer* to me as a bedtime story when I was eleven. I thought Huck and Tom could be a lot of fun, but I dismissed Becky Thatcher as a bore. When I was twelve I invested a nickel at a local garage sale in a book that contained short pieces by Mark Twain. That was where I met Twain's Eve. Now, *that's* more like it, I decided, pleased to meet a female character I could identify *with* instead of against. Eve had spunk. Even if she got a lot wrong, you had to give her credit for trying. "The Man That Corrupted

Hadleyburg" left me giddy with satisfaction: none of my adolescent reveries of getting even with my enemies were half as neat as the plot of the man who got back at that town. "How I Edited an Agricultural Paper" set me off in uncontrollable giggles.

People sometimes told me that I looked like Huck Finn. "It's the freckles," they'd explain — not explaining anything at all. I didn't read *Huckleberry Finn* until junior year in high school in my English class. It was the fall of 1965. I was living in a small town in Connecticut. I expected a sequel to *Tom Sawyer.* So when the teacher handed out the books and announced our assignment, my jaw dropped: "Write a paper on how Mark Twain used irony to attack racism in *Huckleberry Finn.*"

The year before, the bodies of three young men who had gone to Mississippi to help blacks register to vote — James Chaney, Andrew Goodman, and Michael Schwerner — had been found in a shallow grave; a group of white segregationists (the county sheriff among them) had been arrested in connection with the murders. America's inner cities were simmering with pent-up rage that began to explode in the summer of 1965, when riots in Watts left thirty-four people dead. None of this made any sense to me. I was confused, angry, certain that there was something missing from the news stories I read each day: the why. Then I met Pap Finn. And the Phelpses.

Pap Finn, Huck tells us, "had been drunk over in town" and "was just all mud." He erupts into a drunken tirade about "a free nigger ... from Ohio — a mulatter, most as white as a white man," with "the whitest shirt on you ever see, too, and the shiniest hat; and there ain't a man in town that's got as fine clothes as what he had."

> ... they said he was a p'fessor in a college, and could talk all kinds of languages, and knowed everything. And that ain't the wust. They said he could *vote*, when he was at home. Well, that let me out. Thinks I, what is the country a-coming to? It was 'lection day, and I was just about to go and vote, myself, if I warn't too drunk to get there; but when they told me there was a State in this country where they'd let that nigger vote, I drawed out. I says I'll never vote agin. Them's the very words I said.... And to see the

cool way of that nigger — why, he wouldn't a give me the road if I hadn't
shoved him out o' the way.[12]

Later on in the novel, when the runaway slave Jim gives up his freedom to
nurse a wounded Tom Sawyer, a white doctor testifies to the stunning altru-
ism of his actions. The Phelpses and their neighbors, all fine, upstanding,
well-meaning, churchgoing folk,

> agreed that Jim had acted very well, and was deserving to have some notice
> took of it, and reward. So every one of them promised, right out and
> hearty, that they wouldn't curse him no more.
>
> Then they come out and locked him up. I hoped they was going to say
> he could have one or two of the chains took off, because they was rotten
> heavy, or could have meat and greens with his bread and water, but they
> didn't think of it.[13]

Why did the behavior of these people tell me more about why Watts
burned than anything I had read in the daily paper? And why did a drunk
Pap Finn railing against a black college professor from Ohio whose vote was
as good as his own tell me more about white anxiety over black political
power than anything I had seen on the evening news?

Mark Twain knew that there was nothing, absolutely *nothing*, a black man
could do — including selflessly sacrificing his freedom, the only thing of value
he had — that would make white society see beyond the color of his skin. And
Mark Twain knew that depicting racists with chilling accuracy would expose
the viciousness of their world view like nothing else could. It was an insight
echoed some eighty years after Mark Twain penned Pap Finn's rantings
about the black professor, when Malcolm X famously asked, "Do you know
what white racists call black Ph.D.'s?" and answered, "'*Nigger!*'"[14]

Mark Twain taught me things I needed to know. He taught me to understand the raw racism that lay behind what I saw on the evening news. He
taught me that the most well-meaning people can be hurtful and myopic. He
taught me to recognize the supreme irony of a country founded in freedom
that continued to deny freedom to so many of its citizens. Every time I hear of

another effort to kick Huck Finn out of school somewhere, I recall everything that Mark Twain taught *this* high school junior, and I find myself jumping into the fray.[15] I remember the black high school student who called CNN during the phone-in portion of a 1985 debate between Dr. John Wallace, a black educator spearheading efforts to ban the book, and myself. She accused Dr. Wallace of insulting her and all black high school students by suggesting they weren't smart enough to understand Mark Twain's irony. And I recall the black cameraman on the *CBS Morning News* who came up to me after he finished shooting another debate between Dr. Wallace and myself. He said he had never read the book by Mark Twain that we had been arguing about — but now he really wanted to. One thing that puzzled him, though, was why a white woman was defending it and a black man was attacking it, because as far as he could see from what we'd been saying, the book made whites look pretty bad.

As I came to understand *Huckleberry Finn* and *Pudd'nhead Wilson* as commentaries on the era now known as the nadir of American race relations, those books pointed me toward the world recorded in nineteenth-century black newspapers and periodicals and in fiction by Mark Twain's black contemporaries. My investigation of the role black voices and traditions played in shaping Mark Twain's art helped make me aware of their role in shaping all of American culture.[16] My research underlined for me the importance of changing the stories we tell about who we are to reflect the realities of what we've been.[17]

Ever since our encounter in high school English, Mark Twain has shown me the potential of American literature and American history to illuminate each other. Rarely have I found a contradiction or complexity we grapple with as a nation that Mark Twain had not puzzled over as well. He insisted on taking America seriously. And he insisted on *not* taking America seriously: "I think that there is but a single specialty with us, only one thing that can be called by the wide name 'American,'" he once wrote. "That is the national devotion to ice-water."[18]

Mark Twain threw back at us our dreams and our denial of those dreams, our greed, our goodness, our ambition, and our laziness, all rattling around together in that vast echo chamber of our talk — that sharp, spunky American talk that Mark Twain figured out how to write down without robbing it of its energy and immediacy. Talk shaped by voices that the official arbiters of "culture" deemed of no importance — voices of children, voices of slaves, voices of servants, voices of ordinary people. Mark Twain listened. And he made us listen. To the stories he told us, and to the truths they conveyed. He still has a lot to say that we need to hear.

Mark Twain lives — in our libraries, classrooms, homes, theaters, movie houses, streets, and most of all in our speech. His optimism energizes us, his despair sobers us, and his willingness to keep wrestling with the hilarious and horrendous complexities of it all keeps us coming back for more. As the twenty-first century approaches, may he continue to goad us, chasten us, delight us, berate us, and cause us to erupt in unrestrained laughter in unexpected places.

NOTES

1. Ernest Hemingway, *Green Hills of Africa* (New York: Charles Scribner's Sons, 1935), 22. George Bernard Shaw to Samuel L. Clemens, July 3, 1907, quoted in Albert Bigelow Paine, *Mark Twain: A Biography* (New York: Harper and Brothers, 1912), 3:1398.

2. Allen Carey-Webb, "Racism and *Huckleberry Finn*: Censorship, Dialogue and Change," *English Journal* 82, no. 7 (November 1993):22.

3. See Louis J. Budd, "Impersonators," in J. R. LeMaster and James D. Wilson, eds., *The Mark Twain Encyclopedia* (New York: Garland Publishing Company, 1993), 389–91.

4. See Shelley Fisher Fishkin, "Ripples and Reverberations," part 3 of *Lighting Out for the Territory: Reflections on Mark Twain and American Culture* (New York: Oxford University Press, 1996).

5. There are two exceptions. Twain published chapters from his autobiography in the *North American Review* in 1906 and 1907, but this material was not published in book form in Twain's lifetime; our volume reproduces the material as it appeared in the *North American Review*. The other exception is our final volume, *Mark Twain's Speeches*, which appeared two months after Twain's death in 1910.

An unauthorized handful of copies of *1601* was privately printed by an Alexander Gunn of Cleveland at the instigation of Twain's friend John Hay in 1880. The first American edition authorized by Mark Twain, however, was printed at the United States Military Academy at West Point in 1882; that is the edition reproduced here.

XXVIII : SHELLEY FISHER FISHKIN

It should further be noted that four volumes — *The Stolen White Elephant and Other Detective Stories, Following the Equator and Anti-imperialist Essays, The Diaries of Adam and Eve, and 1601, and Is Shakespeare Dead?* — bind together material originally published separately. In each case the first American edition of the material is the version that has been reproduced, always in its entirety. Because Twain constantly recycled and repackaged previously published works in his collections of short pieces, a certain amount of duplication is unavoidable. We have selected volumes with an eye toward keeping this duplication to a minimum.

Even the twenty-nine-volume Oxford Mark Twain has had to leave much out. No edition of Twain can ever claim to be "complete," for the man was too prolix, and the file drawers of both ephemera and as yet unpublished texts are deep.

6. With the possible exception of *Mark Twain's Speeches*. Some scholars suspect Twain knew about this book and may have helped shape it, although no hard evidence to that effect has yet surfaced. Twain's involvement in the production process varied greatly from book to book. For a fuller sense of authorial intention, scholars will continue to rely on the superb definitive editions of Twain's works produced by the Mark Twain Project at the University of California at Berkeley as they become available. Dense with annotation documenting textual emendation and related issues, these editions add immeasurably to our understanding of Mark Twain and the genesis of his works.

7. Except for a few titles that were not in its collection. The American Antiquarian Society in Worcester, Massachusetts, provided the first edition of *King Leopold's Soliloquy*; the Elmer Holmes Bobst Library of New York University furnished the 1906–7 volumes of the *North American Review* in which *Chapters from My Autobiography* first appeared; the Harry Ransom Humanities Research Center at the University of Texas at Austin made their copy of the West Point edition of *1601* available; and the Mark Twain Project provided the first edition of *Extract from Captain Stormfield's Visit to Heaven.*

8. The specific copy photographed for Oxford's facsimile edition is indicated in a note on the text at the end of each volume.

9. All quotations from contemporary writers in this essay are taken from their introductions to the volumes of The Oxford Mark Twain, and the quotations from Mark Twain's works are taken from the texts reproduced in The Oxford Mark Twain.

10. *The Diaries of Adam and Eve*, The Oxford Mark Twain [hereafter OMT] (New York: Oxford University Press, 1996), p. 33.

11. *Tom Sawyer Abroad*, OMT, p. 74.

12. *Adventures of Huckleberry Finn*, OMT, p. 49–50.

13. Ibid., p. 358.

14. Malcolm X, *The Autobiography of Malcolm X*, with the assistance of Alex Haley (New York: Grove Press, 1965), p. 284.

15. I do not mean to minimize the challenge of teaching this difficult novel, a challenge for which all teachers may not feel themselves prepared. Elsewhere I have developed some concrete strategies for approaching the book in the classroom, including teaching it in the context of the history of American race relations and alongside books by black writers. See Shelley Fisher Fishkin, "Teaching *Huckleberry Finn*," in James S. Leonard, ed., *Making Mark Twain Work in the Classroom* (Durham: Duke University Press, forthcoming). See also Shelley Fisher Fishkin, *Was Huck Black? Mark Twain and African-American Voices* (New York: Oxford University Press, 1993), pp. 106–8, and a curriculum kit in preparation at the Mark Twain House in Hartford, containing teaching suggestions from myself, David Bradley, Jocelyn Chadwick-Joshua, James Miller, and David E. E. Sloane.

16. See Fishkin, *Was Huck Black?* See also Fishkin, "Interrogating 'Whiteness,' Complicating 'Blackness': Remapping American Culture," in Henry Wonham, ed., *Criticism and the Color Line: Desegregating American Literary Studies* (New Brunswick: Rutgers UP, 1996, pp. 251–90 and in shortened form in *American Quarterly* 47, no. 3 (September 1995):428–66.

17. I explore the roots of my interest in Mark Twain and race at greater length in an essay entitled "Changing the Story," in Jeffrey Rubin-Dorsky and Shelley Fisher Fishkin, eds., *People of the Book: Thirty Scholars Reflect on Their Jewish Identity* (Madison: U of Wisconsin Press, 1996), pp. 47–63.

18. "What Paul Bourget Thinks of Us," *How to Tell a Story and Other Essays*, OMT, p. 197.

INTRODUCTION
Charles Johnson

In the first book of his five-volume study of western philosophy, *The Classical Mind*, W. T. Jones observed, "The central problem of culture is to reconcile the mechanistic, nonteleological view of nature, which Atomism first formulated and which modern science has largely adopted, with an ethical, religious, and humanistic conception of man. . . . The whole history of philosophy since the seventeenth century is in fact hardly more than a series of variations on this central theme."

At the heart of these perspectives on our experience — determinism versus free will, essence versus existence — is our realization that as human subjects our relationship to our bodies is often that of radical otherness. We know ourselves to be physical creatures, our bodies *objects* that occur in a world of *things*, and we know that the flesh can be approached quantitatively, measured and analyzed in strictly material terms. How often have we heard that on the market our bodies are worth no more than a dollar or two in chemicals, reducible to five pounds of minerals, one pound of carbohydrates, a quarter ounce of vitamins, and a few pounds of protein? As material beings, our bodies and brains both obey the laws of physics, the caprice of nature, accident and chance, and for this modern, materialist orientation we are to a very large degree indebted to the bifurcation of man into mind-substance (*res cogitantes*) and body-substance (*res extensae*) by René Descartes, who regarded animals as no more than machines, their behavior based almost entirely on external stimuli, and their learning, (if it can be called that) so directly determined by past experience that we can all but predict how they will conduct themselves in the present and future. As philosopher Don Ihde points out in *Existential Technics*, "From Descartes on, the 'world' has frequently been characterized as a 'mechanism' which at one time was sometimes tinkered with by the Maker — but which today runs without tinkering. Even our bodies and those of animals were, and continue to be, interpreted along *technological* lines. We are contrivances of pumps (hearts), levers (arms), and electrical systems (nerves)."

But even when we admit, "I am my body," and even if we allow that the creations of our own hand — the machine and computer — can be seen as its analogue, we nevertheless feel that we are *not* merely matter blindly subservient to natural forces beyond our will; we feel the self (or soul) cannot be reduced to the empirical objects of physics, chemistry, or neurology, and this persistent belief in the primacy of consciousness over a purely naturalistic interpretation of being finds its finest expression in the world's great religions as well as in the better texts of modern humanism.

Neither view is wrong. These are age-old antinomies, and depending upon the evidence selected, either orientation can be compellingly (yet only provisionally) argued. Phenomenologist Paul Ricoeur defines the problem succinctly in *Fallible Man* when he says, "It is possible for man to take two divergent and nonreconcilable perspectives upon himself because within man there is a non-coincidence which is that of the *finite* and the *infinite*," or of the physical and the mental.

It is not surprising that these two perspectives, often at war within a single consciousness, are the interlocutors that Mark Twain sets to debating one another in *What Is Man?* How could one of America's greatest storytellers ignore a theme central to western culture since the seventeenth century, or fail to wonder about its implications for good and evil? In the book's preface, Twain states his belief that "millions upon millions of men" have struggled with this problem, reached his conclusions, and remained silent "because they dreaded (*and could not bear*) the disapproval of the people around them." Nor is it surprising that Twain chose to present his views through the Socratic dialogue, a dramatic strategy particularly useful in dealing with antinomies because it gives an author the advantage of splitting himself into two selves, as it were: an Old Man, a Young Man. With this device Twain could explore these "non-reconcilable perspectives" by in effect arguing with himself, taking now the romantic side of the naive young idealist, now that of the elder apparently advocating a mechanistic vision of the world in a funny, frequently hilarious conversation sprung from the cranky thesis that "the human being is merely a machine, and nothing more" (3). However, what does surprise us and pique our curiosity is our discovery that Twain put off publishing this book for many years, and then only released it in a limited edition of two hundred and fifty copies.

H. L. Mencken, thinking he understood the reason for Twain's hesitancy and long delay, wrote in a 1919 essay, "His own speculations always half-appalled him. . . . He was not only afraid to utter what he believed; he was even a bit timorous about *believing* what he believed." For this critic, Twain's fear of making public his hundred-forty-page rumination on human nature ("a book representing him more accurately than any other, both as artist and as man," says Mencken) is understandable to the degree that "Mark knew his countrymen; he knew their intense suspicion of ideas" that openly challenged American religious and social prejudices.

On at least one point Mencken is right. These are hardly ideas that at first blush will win instant converts, though Twain's ultimate goal, I believe, was not to produce in *What Is Man?* a work that might satisfy the philosophers (it won't, despite his best efforts, and perhaps he was reluctant to publish in part because he knew this), but rather to make the strongest possible statement about human vanity — a statement that by the book's conclusion, far from being at odds with Christian piety, is overwhelmingly supportive of it.

In her afterword to this volume, Linda Wagner-Martin reminds us that Twain's dialogue "was not meant to be fun. Or funny. Or a mere pastime. It was intended to be what it was, a fairly rigorous philosophical exercise." So let us examine its rigor, one proposition at a time.

Twain's Old Man bases his argument on a tenuous analogy between men and steam engines (and not just ordinary steam engines, but a variety the Old Man manages to concoct from stone), establishing no more than a whimsical, metaphoric connection between the two. He and the Young Man are unaware that his comparison comes dangerously close to the Fallacy of Division (assuming the parts of anything are the same as the whole). After this confusing choice of metaphor, the Old Man hurries to the first principle in his "infernal philosophy": "Whatsoever a man is, is due to his *make*, and to the *influences* brought to bear upon it by his heredities, his habitat, his associations. He is moved, directed, COMMANDED, by exterior influences — *solely*. He originates nothing, not even a thought" (7). Against the Young Man's feeble objections, Twain's country metaphysician counters that "personally you cannot claim even the slender merit of *putting the borrowed materials together*. That was done *automatically* — by your mental machinery, in strict accordance with the law of that machinery's construction. And you not only did not make that machinery yourself, but you have *not even any command over it*" (8).

Like the Young Man, we listen attentively, leaning forward in our chairs, wetting our throats perhaps with whiskey, chewing on these statements, and remembering that, yes, Kant's *Critique of Pure Reason* makes credible the claim that in its operations the mind imposes form upon our perceptions as a means of making spatial and temporal experience itself possible. And psychology, we recall, suggests discernible patterns in thought processes, patterns over which we have no control, at least in the Freudian tradition, and which are based on external influences, environment, perhaps even sensations far below our level of conscious awareness.

Yet something here feels very wrong. "No man ever originates anything," the Old Man insists. "All his thoughts, all his impulses, come *from the outside*" (10). This claim in a single sentence eliminates Kantian *a priori* judgments, necessary and universal, that come to us independent of external influences — for example, our knowing that the interior angles of a triangle must equal two right angles. The Old Man, expanding on his description of the machinelike operations of the mind in part 5, in a section called "The Thinking-Process," says, "Men observe and combine, that is all. So does a rat" (94). He leaves no room whatsoever for abstract thinking — observing many trees, for example, then forming a thesis about trees as such, which is the very type of exercise in reason that makes the Old Man's general theorizing about "man" possible, and of which the rat with its less complex mental "machinery" is incapable, as far as we know.

And regarding the Old Man's insistence that the brain is "merely a machine; and it works automatically, not by will power. *It has no command over itself, its owner has no command over it,*" we eagerly wait for the Young Man to raise his hand in objection, replying that far from the scene of their conversation, in India, there is a tradition of yoga as old a Patanjali, and a practice called meditation (*dhyana*) based on rigorous exercises in concentrated control of the senses (*dharana*) intended to achieve precisely the mastery over thought, regulation of emotional response, and deconditioning from undesirable past influences that the Old Man has so emphatically and dogmatically denied (11).

Unfortunately, Twain's Young Man knows nothing of cultural traditions that swept through the east and have no western parallel. And even for the reader untrained in any philosophical tradition, he caves in far too soon when he should be offering alternative metaphors and demanding that the Old Man define foundational and soon to become troublesome terms such as a man's "make." Instead, he offers no resistance as the Old Man reduces Shakespeare to a "a Gobelin loom" (11), qualifies his theme of determinism a bit by allowing for the virtue of "*training in right directions*" (13), and proceeds to outline a phenomenologically stronger yet no less provocative law for man's psychological life: the ego-deflating "Gospel of Self Approval" (39).

In a word, Twain's "gospel," the centerpiece concept in his theory of human nature, is an argument for self-interest based on the simple observation that men pursue pleasure and avoid pain at all cost. "From his cradle to his grave a man never does a single thing which has any FIRST AND FOREMOST object but one — to secure peace of mind, spiritual comfort, for HIMSELF" (21). "Make" — loosely defined as character and conscience — determines the specific form of this "Master Impulse" within each and every human mind, insuring that any given individual "always looks out for Number One — *first*" (27). On the surface, says the Old Man, and before proper reflection, a deed may seem, as the Young Man puts it, "noble . . . beautiful; its grace . . . marred by no fleck or blemish or suggestion of self-interest," but behind the virtues we have for centuries called love, selflessness, charity, magnanimity, and forgiveness lurks the fact that these are nothing more than forms of self-gratification. A man gives a beggar his last coin, not because he is compassionate or generous, but rather because the suffering he would experience, inflicted by his conscience (or childhood upbringing or public disapproval), would be greater if he turned away. "Thinking of *his* pain . . . he must buy relief from that," says the Old Man (20). "A man cannot be comfortable without *his own* approval" (23).

This "iron law," according to Twain's philosopher, covers all cases of human behavior: the mother goes naked to clothe her child for her sake, not the child's; a white slave master frees his Negro bondsman for his own sake — so *he* can sleep peacefully at night — rather than, "first and foremost," for any idealistic principle such as justice or Christian mercy. And because man "performs but one duty — the duty of contenting his spirit, the duty of making himself agreeable to himself," some people will even gladly choose death over life to appease the Master Impulse to feel good about themselves (26). In the Old Man's metaphysic, "*None but gods have ever had a thought which did not come from the outside*" (10), which casts men as slaves shaped by their social conditioning (i.e., the ideas of other men and women), specifically by a super-ego (to use a Freudian term Twain did not know) that deprives them of peace when they betray this impulse. Thus, even self-sacrifice "describes a thing which does not exist" (37).

Does the Old Man's determinism and his giving primacy to the pleasure principle seem familiar? It should, for it has its origin in the so-called enlightened hedonism of the Greek atomist Epicurus, who wrote:

> For it is to obtain this end that we always act, namely, to avoid pain and fear. . . . And for this cause we call pleasure the beginning and end of the blessed life. For we recognize pleasure as the first good innate in us, and from pleasure we begin every act of choice and avoidance, and to pleasure we return again, using the feeling as the standard by which we judge every good.

And since pleasure is the first good and natural to us, for this very reason we do not choose every pleasure, but sometimes we pass over many pleasures, when greater discomfort accrues to us as the result of them: and similarly we think many pains better than pleasures, since a greater pleasure comes to us when we have endured pains for a long time. Every pleasure then because of its natural kinship to us is good, yet not every pleasure is to be chosen: even as every pain also is an evil, yet not all are always of a nature to be avoided. Yet by a scale of comparison and by the consideration of advantages and disadvantages we must form our judgement on all these matters.

Completeness in any analysis of the hoary pain-pleasure hypothesis as the universal and primary human motivation requires us to raise one further objection: What of the pathological mind? Does pleasure or "peace of mind" always follow, for example, the deeds of a murderer, a serial killer? Why, then, do many express contrition even after severe sentences, with no hope of leniency? Narratives provided by such men, many of whom state that their actions have *only* brought pain, point to a conclusion contrary to that of the Old Man and Epicurus.

Our Young Man knows well enough that if he can find but one counter-example to the Gospel of Self-Approval, he will be able to free himself from the tyranny of the Old Man's *idée fixe*. Sadly, he can think of none, for the explanation based on self-interest does in fact seem to account for some substantial portion of human behavior. Yet and still, the Old Man's ideas are far from systematic, coherent, consistent, or complete. In part 4, devoted to "Training," he portrays men as lacking an inherent sense of good and evil, and the mind as something like John Locke's *tabula rasa*, insisting again that a man "gets *all* his ideas, all his impressions, from the outside" (62). However, he soon adds to training another major influence, "*temperament* — that is, the disposition you were born with. *You can't eradicate your disposition nor any rag of it. . . .* You have a warm temper? . . . You will never get rid of it" (69). Both he and the Young Man disguise from themselves the difficulty this inclusion of nature adds to the earlier argument based on nurture.

For example, in part 3, the Old Man considers the case of more than a thousand soldiers who went down with their troop ship so that the women and children aboard could have the lifeboats. Why? Because they were compelled by the training, associations, and environment that produced "a soldier's pride, a soldier's self-respect, a soldier's ideals," in other words, a soldier's superego (52). But having admitted the potency of temperament, don't we undermine the extent to which training can shape the self-interested dictates of the "Interior Master"? It would seem so, for in the book's conclusion, the Old Man grumps, "Beliefs? Mere beliefs? Mere convictions? They are powerless. They strive in vain against inborn temperament" (136). He goes on to add, "Beliefs are *acquirements*, temperaments are *born*; beliefs are subject to change, nothing whatever can change temperament" (138). Little wonder the Young Man is confused.

More damaging to his argument, at least to twentieth-century eyes, is part 6, where "Instinct and Thought" are discussed, initially in an outrageous and, I believe, intentionally funny way, when the Old Man refuses to put men and rats on the same moral level because it "would not be fair to the rat. The rat is well above [man], there" (99). But problems soon arise when the Old Man observes, "I think that the rat's mind and the man's mind are the same machine, but of unequal capacities — like yours and Edison's; like the African pigmy's and Homer's; like the Bushman's and Bismarck's" (100). Here racial essentialism rears its ugly nineteenth-century head in Twain's understanding of a man's "make." Not much later the Old Man adds, "As a thinker and planner the ant is the equal of any savage race of men; as a self-educated specialist in several arts she is the superior of any savage race of men" (106).

The author of *What Is Man?* could not, I fear, escape the pitfall that awaits anyone who attempts to be strictly empirical or scientific when addressing human nature; at best what is achieved is pseudoscience, or in our own time, an essentialism based on genetics or dubious findings relating race to test scores, as in Herrnstein and Murray's controversial study, *The Bell Curve*.

Equally thorny is the section called "A Difficult Question," in which the Young Man says, "Now when *I* speak of a man, he is *the whole thing in one,* and easy to hold and contemplate" (123). By this he means precisely what we all experience when we contemplate our embodiment — that we never experience ourselves as, say, a chemical process, or in the terms we apply to machines. Much like David Hume in a *Treatise of Human Nature*, where a radically empirical approach is used to deny the existence of the self and to question even causation, the Old Man replies, "We all use the 'I' in this indeterminate fashion, there is no help for it. We imagine a Master and King over what you call The Whole Thing, and we speak of him as 'I,' but when we try to define him we find we cannot do it" (126). Neither an "I" nor the soul can be apprehended through direct perception. The self or soul is not given as an object during the moment of sensation. The Old Man shares this view not only with Hume but also with early Buddhist thinkers. Yet the epistemological and ontological implications of this denial of personal identity for the Gospel of Self-Approval are not pursued. (If there is no "I," if it is an illusion, then the Master Impulse surely must be illusory too.)

Throughout the dialogue, the Old Man's young apprentice blinks away such questions, and we are willing to put them aside momentarily because in part 4 it becomes clear that the elder speaker has patched these different ideas together in order to bring us to more pressing ethical concerns — the moral issue of "right living" that no doubt led Twain to compose *What Is Man?* in the first place. In his "Admonition," the Old Man says to the Young Man, "Diligently train your ideals *upward* and *still upward* toward a summit where you will find your chiefest pleasure in conduct which, while contenting you, will be sure to confer benefits upon your neighbor and the community"(71). It is, he admits, a prescription taught by the world's great religions, "all the great gospels," but with this difference: there are no delusions about why moral acts are performed — men put their comfort first, always, and the good of others second. But what other "gospels" is the Old Man referring to? I would guess one to be the utilitarian social philosophy of Jeremy Bentham, whose "moral calculus" and Principle of Utility the Old Man seems to echo on several points.

"Nature has placed mankind under the governance of two sovereign masters, *Pleasure and Pain*," wrote Bentham.

To them . . . we refer all our decisions, every resolve that we make in life. The man who affects to have withdrawn himself from their despotic sway does not know what he is talking about. To seek pleasure and to shun pain is his sole aim, even at the moment when he is denying himself the greatest enjoyment and courting penalties the most severe. . . . *The Principle of Utility*, accordingly, consists in taking as our starting-point, in every process of ordered reasoning, the calculus or comparative estimate of pains and pleasures.

And this principle is said to insure, as the Old Man hopes, that a man's pursuit of pleasure will result in some measure of good for others.

It cannot be said that Twain was an original or groundbreaking thinker in *What Is Man?* (Mencken attributes the bulk of his ideas to the nineteenth century's "Great Agnostic," Robert G. Ingersoll.) He overreaches himself when he takes on one of the most difficult questions in intellectual history, a question for which we do not have a satisfactory answer to this very day. But his motives, it seems to me, are ultimately ethical ones, even religious and political ones.

The Young Man sees it otherwise, lamenting at the end of their conversation that the Old Man has set forth

a desolating doctrine; it is not inspiring, enthusing, uplifting. It takes the glory out of man, it takes the pride out of him, it takes the heroism out of him, it denies him all personal credit, all applause; it not only degrades him to a machine, but allows him no control over the machine; makes a mere coffee-mill of him, and neither permits him to supply the coffee nor turn the crank; his sole and piteously humble function being to grind coarse or fine, according to his make, outside impulses doing all the rest. (132)

He does not see that what the Old Man has taken from humankind he has given to God, though he should have been alerted to the spiritual *telos* of the conversation when in the section entitled "Not Two Values, but Only One," the Old Man, despite his seemingly materialist and mechanistic perspective, declares, "There are no *material* values, there are only spiritual ones" — a point anticipated in the earlier discussion of men and rats, for whose achievements alike, he says, "the whole credit belongs to their Maker. They are entitled to no honors, no praises, no monuments when they die, no remembrance." For all its playfulness with ideas, *What Is Man?* boils down, in the final analysis, to a scathing critique of human vanity, a subject Twain turned to often in his fiction. His entire argument, one might say, is encapsulated in a single, revealing exchange.

o.m.: ... does man manufacture any one of those seeds, or are they all born in him?

y.m.: Born in him.

o.m.: Who manufactures them, then?

y.m.: God.

o.m.: Where does the credit of it belong?

y.m.: To God.

o.m.: And the glory of which you spoke, and the applause?

y.m.: To God.

o.m.: Then it is *you* who degrade man. You make him claim glory, praise, flattery, for every valuable thing he possesses — *borrowed* finery, the whole of it; no rag of it earned by himself, not a detail of it produced by his own labor. *You* make man a humbug; have I done worse by him?"

y.m.: You have made a machine of him.

o.m.: Who devised that cunning and beautiful mechanism, a man's hand?

y.m.: God.

o.m.: Who devised the law by which it automatically hammers out of a piano an elaborate piece of music, without error, while the man is thinking about something else, or talking to a friend?

y.m.: God.

o.m.: Who devised the blood? Who devised the wonderful machinery which automatically drives its renewing and refreshing streams through the body, day and night, without assistance or advice from the man? Who devised the man's mind, whose machinery works automatically, interests itself in what it pleases, regardless of his will or desire, labors all night when it likes, deaf to his appeals for mercy? God devised all these thing [sic]. *I* have not made man a machine, God made him a machine. (133–35)

Not once in *What Is Man?* does the Old Man apply his reductive, empirical logic to the existence of God, as he did to the soul, the "I," and the virtues. For both interlocutors the Maker is a given to whom all praises belong, as in the biblical words "Not I but the Father within me doeth the works." But once he opens *this* door in the conversation, the conclusion — and intellectual quandaries — become all too evident, whether the Old Man admits them or not. "Temperament" and "make," all the external influences of the world that create the conditions for man as a machine, have come from the Maker. No form of determinism could be greater than this. All the internal evidence in the dialogue suggests that the Old Man's portrait of God is as the watchmaker who has created in man and the world a delicate mechanism left to run on its own ("God makes a man with honest and dishonest *possibilities* in him and stops there," the Old Man tells us), and this empirically unacceptable resting place for the Old Man's "drunken theories" summarily deposits readers in the realm of theological dilemmas two millennia old — Why has God chosen to make men like machines? What evidence is there even for a Maker? — that the dialogue does not wish to confront. In the end, *What Is Man?* impales itself on *both* horns of the conflicting views described by W. T. Jones — the mechanistic *and* the ethical and religious — yet does real justice to neither.

On the other hand, the Humean conclusion concerning the "I," while hardly a new idea, is certainly a daring, even a revolutionary one for an author releasing his work to American audiences in 1906. Similarly, we can endlessly revisit the dour Gospel of Self-Approval, and respect it for its cantankerous honesty. Just as we can respect the Old Man's pessimism about institutional religion and government, which makes him rail in the book's final speech about

a thousand wild and tame religions, every kind of government that can be thought of, from tiger to house-cat, each nation *knowing* it has the only true religion and the only sane system of government, each despising all the

others, each an ass and not suspecting it, each proud of its fancied supremacy, each perfectly sure it is the pet of God, each with undoubting
confidence summoning Him to take command in time of war, each surprised when He goes over to the enemy, . . . in a word, the whole human
race content, always content, persistently content, indestructibly content,
happy, thankful, proud, *no matter what its religion is, nor whether its master be a tiger or house-cat.* (139–40)

Nevertheless, we come to the end of Twain's dialogue wishing the author
had been better acquainted with western and eastern intellectual history. We
are saddened that he paid so little attention to contradictory statements in his
text, and in our ears we hear Mencken's harsh judgment: "There is more to
the making of literature than the mere depiction of human beings at their ob-
scene follies; there is also the play of ideas." Mencken faulted Twain for his
timidity about publishing this book and for not trusting his own ideas, concluding that this "weakness takes a good deal from his stature. It leaves him
radiating a subtle flavor of the second-rate. With more courage, he would
have gone a great deal further, and left a far deeper mark upon the intellectual
history of his time."

To his credit, however, Twain leavens his philosophical dialogue with rich
moments of humor and anecdote, and in part 5 he wonderfully turns this entire book on its head when the Old Man, distancing himself from Diogenes,
confesses, "I said I have been a Truth-Seeker. . . . I am not that now" (95).
True to his eccentric belief that men are like automatons, he does not exclude
himself from his philosophy's condemnations.

Having found the Truth; perceiving that beyond question man has but one
moving impulse — the contenting of his own spirit — and is merely a machine and entitled to no personal merit for anything he does, it is not humanly possible for me to seek further. The rest of my days will be spent in
patching and painting and puttying and caulking my priceless possession
and in looking the other way when an imploring argument or a damaging
fact approaches. (96)

There is little here that we can accept as self-evident, unarguable, or semi-nal for philosophic thought. But while Mark Twain may not have been able to unveil man's nature in intellectually satisfactory terms, the brilliant author of fiction masterpieces like *Huckleberry Finn* and *A Connecticut Yankee in King Arthur's Court* nevertheless created in *What Is Man?* two memorable and thoroughly consistent characters who entertain us from the first page to the last, and more importantly, force us to ponder — as Twain apparently did for much of his life — one of the enduring mysteries of human existence on earth.

WHAT IS MAN?

WHAT IS MAN?

WHAT IS MAN?

NEW YORK
PRINTED AT THE DE VINNE PRESS
1906

FEBRUARY, 1905. The studies for these papers were begun twenty-five or twenty-seven years ago. The papers were written seven years ago. I have examined them once or twice per year since and found them satisfactory. I have just examined them again, and am still satisfied that they speak the truth.

Every thought in them has been thought (and accepted as unassailable truth) by millions upon millions of men—and concealed, kept private. Why did they not speak out? Because they dreaded (*and could not bear*) the disapproval of the people around them. Why have not I published? The same reason has restrained me, I think. I can find no other.

WHAT IS MAN?

I

a. *Man the Machine.* b. *Personal Merit.*

[The Old Man and the Young Man had been conversing. The Old Man had asserted that the human being is merely a machine, and nothing more. The Young Man objected, and asked him to go into particulars and furnish his reasons for his position.]

OLD MAN. What are the materials of which a steam-engine is made?

YOUNG MAN. Iron, steel, brass, white-metal, and so on.

O. M. Where are these found?

Y. M. In the rocks.

O. M. In a pure state?

Y. M. No—in ores.

O. M. Are the metals suddenly deposited in the ores?

Y. M. No—it is the patient work of countless ages.

O. M. You could make the engine out of the rocks themselves?

Y. M. Yes, a brittle one and not valuable.

O. M. You would not require much, of such an engine as that?

Y. M. No—substantially nothing.

O. M. To make a fine and capable engine, how would you proceed?

Y. M. Drive tunnels and shafts into the hills; blast out the iron ore; crush it, smelt it, reduce it to pig-iron; put some of it through the Bessemer process and make steel of it. Mine and treat and combine the several metals of which brass is made.

O. M. Then?

Y. M. Out of the perfected result, build the fine engine.

O. M. You would require much of this one?

Y. M. Oh, indeed yes.

O. M. It could drive lathes, drills, planers, punches, polishers, in a word all the cunning machines of a great factory?

Y. M. It could.

O. M. What could the stone engine do?

Y. M. Drive a sewing-machine, possibly—nothing more, perhaps.

O. M. Men would admire the other engine and rapturously praise it?

Y. M. Yes.

O. M. But not the stone one?

Y. M. No.

O. M. The merits of the metal machine would be far above those of the stone one?

Y. M. Of course.

O. M. Personal merits?

Y. M. *Personal* merits? How do you mean?

O. M. It would be personally entitled to the credit of its own performance?

Y. M. The engine? Certainly not.

O. M. Why not?

Y. M. Because its performance is not personal. It is a result of the law of its construction. It is not a *merit* that it does the things which it is set to do— it can't *help* doing them.

O. M. And it is not a personal demerit in the stone machine that it does so little?

Y. M. Certainly not. It does no more and no less than the law of its make permits and compels it to do. There is nothing *personal* about it; it cannot choose. In this process of "working up to the matter" is it your idea to work up to the proposition that man and a machine are about the same thing, and that there is no personal merit in the performance of either?

O. M. Yes—but do not be offended; I am meaning no offense. What makes the grand difference between the stone engine and the steel one? Shall we call it training, education? Shall we call the stone engine a savage and the steel one a civilized man? The original rock contained the stuff of which the steel one was built—but along with it a lot of sulphur and stone and other obstructing inborn heredities, brought down from the old geologic ages—prejudices, let us call them. Prejudices which nothing within the rock itself had either *power* to remove or any *desire* to remove. Will you take note of that phrase?

Y. M. Yes. I have written it down: "Prejudices which nothing within the rock itself had either power to remove or any desire to remove." Go on.

O. M. Prejudices which must be removed by *outside influences* or not at all. Put that down.

Y. M. Very well; "Must be removed by outside influences or not at all." Go on.

O. M. The iron's prejudice against ridding itself of the cumbering rock. To make it more exact, the iron's absolute *indifference* as to whether the rock be removed or not. Then comes the *outside influence* and grinds the rock to powder and sets the ore free. The *iron* in the ore is still captive. An *outside influence* smelts it free of the clogging ore. The iron is emancipated iron, now, but indifferent to further progress. An *outside influence* beguiles it into the Bessemer furnace and refines it into steel of the first quality. It is educated, now—its training is complete. And it has reached its limit. By no possible process can it be educated into *gold*. Will you set that down?

Y. M. Yes. "Everything has its limit—iron ore cannot be educated into gold."

O. M. There are gold men, and tin men, and copper men, and leaden men, and steel men, and so on —and each has the limitations of his nature, his heredities, his training and his environment. You can build engines out of each of these metals, and they will all perform, but you must not require the weak ones to do equal work with the strong ones. In each case, to get the best results, you must free the metal from its obstructing prejudicial ores by education—smelting, refining, and so forth.

Y. M. You have arrived at man, now?

O. M. Yes. Man the machine—man the impersonal engine. Whatsoever a man is, is due to his *make*, and to the *influences* brought to bear upon it by his heredities, his habitat, his associations. He is moved, directed, COMMANDED, by *exterior* influences—*solely*. He *originates* nothing, not even a thought.

Y. M. Oh, come! Where did I get my opinion that this which you are talking is all foolishness?

O. M. It is a quite natural opinion—indeed an inevitable opinion—but *you* did not create the materials out of which it is formed. They are odds and ends of thoughts, impressions, feelings, gathered unconsciously from a thousand books, a thousand conversations, and from streams of thought and feeling which have flowed down into your heart and brain out of the hearts and brains of centuries of ancestors. *Personally* you did not create even the smallest microscopic fragment of the materials out of which your opinion is made; and personally you cannot claim even the slender merit of *putting the borrowed materials together.* That was done *automatically*—by your mental machinery, in strict accordance with the law of that machinery's construction. And you not only did not make that machinery yourself, but you have *not even any command over it.*

Y. M. This is too much. You think I could have formed no opinion but that one?

O. M. Spontaneously? No. And *you did not form that one;* your machinery did it for you—automatically and instantly, without reflection or the need of it.

Y. M. Suppose I had reflected? How then?

O. M. Suppose you try?

Y. M. (*After a quarter of an hour.*) I have reflected.

O. M. You mean you have tried to change your opinion—as an experiment?

Y. M. Yes.

O. M. With success?

Y. M. No. It remains the same; it is impossible to change it.

O. M. I am sorry, but you see, yourself, that your mind is merely a machine, nothing more. You have no command over it, it has no command over itself —it is worked *solely from the outside.* That is the law of its make; it is the law of all machines.

Y. M. Can't I *ever* change one of these automatic opinions?

O. M. No. You can't yourself, but *exterior influences* can do it.

Y. M. And exterior ones *only?*

O. M. Yes—exterior ones only.

Y. M. That position is untenable—I may say ludicrously untenable.

O. M. What makes you think so?

Y. M. I don't merely think it, I know it. Suppose I resolve to enter upon a course of thought, and study, and reading, with the deliberate purpose of changing that opinion; and suppose I succeed. *That* is not the work of an exterior impulse, the whole of it is mine and personal; for I originated the project.

O. M. Not a shred of it. *It grew out of this talk with me.* But for that it would never have occurred to you. No man ever originates anything. All his thoughts, all his impulses, come *from the outside.*

Y. M. It's an exasperating subject. The *first* man had original thoughts, anyway; there was nobody to draw from.

O. M. It is a mistake. Adam's thoughts came to him from the outside. *You* have a fear of death. You did not invent that—you got it from outside, from talk and teaching. Adam had no fear of death —none in the world.

Y. M. Yes he had.

O. M. When he was created?

Y. M. No.

O. M. When, then?

Y. M. When he was threatened with it.

O. M. Then it came from the *outside.* Adam is quite big enough; let us not try to make a god of him. *None but gods have ever had a thought which did not come from the outside.* Adam probably had a good head, but it was of no sort of use to him until it was filled up *from the outside.* He was not able to invent the triflingest little thing with it. He had not a shadow of a notion of the difference between good and evil—he had to get the idea *from the outside.* Neither he nor Eve was able to originate the idea that it was immodest to go naked: the knowledge came in with the apple *from the outside.* A man's brain is so constructed that *it can originate nothing whatever.* It can only use material obtained *outside.* It is merely a machine; and it works automatically, not by will power. *It has no command over itself, its owner has no command over it.*

Y. M. Well, never mind Adam: but certainly Shakespeare's creations—

O. M. No, you mean Shakespeare's *imitations.* Shakespeare created nothing. He correctly observed, and he marvelously painted. He exactly portrayed people whom *God* had created; but he created none himself. Let us spare him the slander of charging him with trying. Shakespeare could not create. *He was a machine, and machines do not create.*

Y. M. Where *was* his excellence, then?

O. M. In this. He was not a sewing machine, like you and me, he was a Gobelin loom. The threads and the colors came into him *from the outside;* outside influences, suggestions, *experiences,* (reading, seeing plays, playing plays, borrowing ideas, and so on), framed the patterns in his mind and started up its complex and admirable machinery, and *it automatically* turned out that pictured and gorgeous fabric which still compels the astonishment of the world. If Shakespeare had been born and bred on a barren and unvisited rock in the ocean his mighty intellect would have had no *outside material* to work with, and could have invented none; and *no outside influences,* teachings, mouldings, persuasions, inspirations, of a valuable sort, and could have invented none; and so Shakespeare would have produced nothing. In Turkey he would have produced something—something up to the highest limit of Turkish influences, associations and training. In France he would have produced something better— something up to the highest limit of the French influences and training. In England he rose to the highest limit attainable through the *outside helps afforded by that land's ideals, influences and training.* You and I are but sewing machines. We must turn out what we can; we must do our endeavor and care nothing at all when the unthinking reproach us for not turning out Gobelins.

Y. M. And so we are mere machines! And machines may not boast, nor feel proud of their performance, nor claim personal merit for it, nor applause and praise. It is an infamous doctrine.

O. M. It isn't a doctrine, it is merely a fact.

Y. M. I suppose, then, there is no more merit in being brave than in being a coward?

O. M. *Personal* merit? No. A brave man does not *create* his bravery. He is entitled to no personal credit for possessing it. It is born to him. A baby born with a billion dollars—where is the personal merit in that? A baby born with nothing—where is the personal demerit in that? The one is fawned upon, admired, worshiped, by sycophants, the other is neglected and despised—where is the sense in it?

Y. M. Sometimes a timid man sets himself the task of conquering his cowardice and becoming brave— and succeeds. What do you say to that?

O. M. That it shows the value of *training in right directions over training in wrong ones.* Inestimably valuable is training, influence, education, in right directions—*training one's self-approbation to elevate its ideals.*

Y. M. But as to merit—the personal merit of the victorious coward's project and achievement?

O. M. There isn't any. In the world's view he is

a worthier man than he was before, but *he* didn't achieve the change—the merit of it is not his.

Y. M. Whose then?

O. M. His *make*, and the influences which wrought upon it from the outside.

Y. M. His make?

O. M. Yes. To start with, he was *not* utterly and completely a coward, or the influences would have had nothing to work upon. He was not afraid of a cow, though perhaps of a bull: not afraid of a woman, but afraid of a man. There was something to build upon. There was a *seed*. No seed, no plant. Did he make that seed himself, or was it born in him? It was no merit of *his* that the seed was there.

Y. M. Well, anyway, the idea of *cultivating* it, the resolution to cultivate it, was meritorious, and he originated that.

O. M. He did nothing of the kind. It came whence *all* impulses, good or bad, come—from *outside*. If that timid man had lived all his life in a community of human rabbits; had never read of brave deeds; had never heard speak of them; had never heard anyone praise them nor express envy of the heroes that had done them, he would have had no more idea of bravery than Adam had of modesty, and it could never by any possibility have occurred to him to *resolve* to become brave. He *could not originate the idea*—it had to come to him from the *outside.* And so, when he heard bravery extolled and cowardice derided, it woke him up. He was ashamed. Perhaps his sweetheart turned up her nose and said, "I am told that you arc a coward!" It was not *he* that turned over the new leaf—she did it for him. *He* must not strut around in the merit of it—it is not his.

Y. M. But anyway he reared the plant after she watered the seed.

O. M. No. *Outside influences* reared it. At the command—and trembling,—he marched out into the field—with other soldiers and in the daytime, not alone and in the dark. He had the *influence of example*, he drew courage from his comrades' courage; he was afraid, and wanted to run, but he did not dare; he was *afraid* to run, with all those soldiers looking on. He was progressing, you see—the moral fear of shame had risen superior to the physical fear of harm. By the end of the campaign experience will have taught him that not *all* who go into battle get hurt—an outside influence which will be helpful to him; and he will also have learned how sweet it is to be praised for courage and be huzza'd at with tear-choked voices as the war-worn regiment marches past the worshiping multitude with flags flying and the drums beating. After that he will be as securely brave as any veteran in the army—and there will not be a shade nor suggestion of *personal merit* in it anywhere; it will all have come from the *outside.* The Victoria Cross breeds more heroes than—

Y. M. Hang it, where is the sense in his becoming brave if he is to get no credit for it?

O. M. Your question will answer itself presently. It involves an important detail of man's make which we have not yet touched upon.

Y. M. What detail is that?

O. M. The impulse which moves a person to do things—the only impulse that ever moves a person to do a thing.

Y. M. The *only* one! Is there but one?

O. M. That is all. There is only one.

Y. M. Well, certainly that is a strange enough doctrine. What is the sole impulse that ever moves a person to do a thing?

O. M. The impulse to *content his own spirit*—the *necessity* of contenting his own spirit and *winning its approval.*

Y. M. Oh, come, that won't do!

O. M. Why won't it?

Y. M. Because it puts him in the attitude of always looking out for his own comfort and advantage; whereas an unselfish man often does a thing solely for another person's good when it is a positive disadvantage to himself.

O. M. It is a mistake. The act must do *him* good, FIRST; otherwise he will not do it. He may *think* he is doing it solely for the other person's sake, but it is not so; he is contenting his own spirit *first*—the other person's benefit has to always take *second* place.

Y. M. What a fantastic idea! What becomes of self-sacrifice? Please answer me that.

O. M. What is self-sacrifice?

Y. M. The doing good to another person where no shadow nor suggestion of benefit to one's self can result from it.

II

Man's Sole Impulse—The Securing of His Own Approval

O. M. There have been instances of it—you think?

Y. M. *Instances?* Millions of them!

O. M. You have not jumped to conclusions? You have examined them—critically?

Y. M. They don't need it: the acts themselves reveal the golden impulse back of them.

O. M. For instance?

Y. M. Well, then, for instance. Take the case in the book here. The man lives three miles up-town. It is bitter cold, snowing hard, midnight. He is about to enter the horse-car when a gray and ragged old woman, a touching picture of misery, puts out her lean hand and begs for rescue from hunger and death. The man finds that he has but a quarter in his pocket, but he does not hesitate: he gives it her and trudges home through the storm. There— it is noble, it is beautiful; its grace is marred by no fleck or blemish or suggestion of self-interest.

O. M. What makes you think that?

Y. M. Pray what else could I think? Do you imagine that there is some other way of looking at it?

O. M. Can you put yourself in the man's place and tell me what he felt and what he thought?

Y. M. Easily. The sight of that suffering old face pierced his generous heart with a sharp pain. He could not bear it. He could endure the three-mile walk in the storm, but he could not endure the tortures his conscience would suffer if he turned his back and left that poor old creature to perish. He would not have been able to sleep, for thinking of it.

O. M. What was his state of mind on his way home?

Y. M. It was a state of joy which only the self-sacrificer knows. His heart sang, he was unconscious of the storm.

O. M. He slept well?

Y. M. One cannot doubt it.

O. M. Very well. Now let us add up the details and see how much he got for his twenty-five cents. Let us try to find out the *real* why of his making the investment. In the first place *he* could n't bear the pain which the old suffering face gave him. So he was thinking of *his* pain—this good man. He must buy a salve for it. If he did not succor the old woman *his* conscience would torture him all the way home. Thinking of *his* pain again. He must buy relief from that. If he did n't relieve the old woman *he* would not get any sleep. He must buy some sleep —still thinking of *himself*, you see. Thus, to sum up, he bought himself free of a sharp pain in his heart, he bought himself free of the tortures of a waiting conscience, he bought a whole night's sleep —all for twenty-five cents! It should make Wall street ashamed of itself. On his way home his heart was joyful, and it sang—profit on top of profit! The impulse which moved the man to succor the old woman was—*first*—to *content his own spirit;* secondly, to relieve *her* sufferings. Is it your opinion that men's acts proceed from one central and unchanging and inalterable impulse, or from a variety of impulses?

Y. M. From a variety, of course—some high and fine and noble, others not. What is your opinion?

O. M. That there is but *one* law, one source.

Y. M. That both the noblest impulses and the basest proceed from that one source?

O. M. Yes.

Y. M. Will you put that law into words?

O. M. Yes. This is the law, keep it in your mind.

From his cradle to his grave a man never does a single thing which has any FIRST AND FOREMOST *object but one—to secure peace of mind, spiritual comfort, for* HIMSELF.

Y. M. Come! He never does anything for any one else's comfort, spiritual or physical?

O. M. No. *Except on those distinct terms*—that it shall *first* secure *his own* spiritual comfort. Otherwise he will not do it.

Y. M. It will be easy to expose the falsity of that proposition.

O. M. For instance?

Y. M. Take that noble passion, love of country, patriotism. A man who loves peace and dreads pain, leaves his pleasant home and his weeping family and marches out to manfully expose himself to hunger, cold, wounds and death. Is that seeking spiritual comfort?

O. M. He loves peace and dreads pain?

Y. M. Yes.

O. M. Then perhaps there is something that he loves *more* than he loves peace—*the approval of his neighbors and the public.* And perhaps there is something which he dreads more than he dreads pain—the *disapproval* of his neighbors and the public. If he is sensitive to shame he will go to the field—not because his spirit will be *entirely* comfortable there, but because it will be more comfortable there than it would be if he remained at home. He will always do the thing which will bring him the *most* mental comfort—for that is *the sole law of his life.* He leaves the weeping family behind; he is sorry to make them uncomfortable, but not sorry enough to sacrifice his *own* comfort to secure theirs.

Y. M. Do you really believe that mere public opinion could force a timid and peaceful man to—

O. M. Go to war? Yes—public opinion can force some men to do *anything*.

Y. M. *Anything?*

O. M. Yes—anything.

Y. M. I don't believe that. Can it force a right-principled man to do a wrong thing?

O. M. Yes.

Y. M. Can it force a kind man to do a cruel thing?

O. M. Yes.

Y. M. Give an instance.

O. M. Alexander Hamilton was a conspicuously high-principled man. He regarded duelling as wrong, and as opposed to the teachings of religion —but in deference to *public opinion* he fought a duel. He deeply loved his family, but to buy public approval he treacherously deserted them and threw his life away, ungenerously leaving them to life-long sorrow in order that he might stand well with a foolish world.   In the then condition of the public standards of honor he could not have been comfortable with the stigma upon him of having refused to fight. The teachings of religion, his devotion to his family, his kindness of heart, his high principles, all went for nothing when they stood in the way of his spiritual comfort.   A man will do *anything*, no matter what it is, *to secure his spiritual comfort;* and he can neither be forced nor persuaded to any act which has not that goal for its object.   Hamilton's act was compelled by the inborn necessity of contenting his own spirit; in this it was like all the other acts of his life, and like all the acts of all men's lives.   Do you see where the kernel of the matter lies?   A man cannot be comfortable without *his own* approval.   He will secure the largest share possible of that, at all costs, all sacrifices.

Y. M. A minute ago you said Hamilton fought that duel to get *public* approval.

O. M. I did.   By refusing to fight the duel he would have secured his family's approval and a large share of his own; but the public approval was more valuable in his eyes than all other approvals put together—in the earth or above it; to secure that would furnish him the *most* comfort of mind, the most *self*-approval; so he sacrificed all other values to get it.

Y. M. Some noble souls have refused to fight duels, and have manfully braved the public contempt.

O. M. They acted *according to their make*. They valued their principles and the approval of their families *above* the public approval. They took the thing they valued *most* and let the rest go. They took what would give them the *largest* share of *personal contentment and approval*—a man *always* does. Public opinion cannot force that kind of men to go to the wars. When they go it is for other reasons. Other spirit-contenting reasons.

Y. M. Always spirit-contenting reasons?

O. M. There are no others.

Y. M. When a man sacrifices his life to save a little child from a burning building, what do you call that?

O. M. When he does it, it is the law of *his* make. *He* can't bear to see the child in that peril, (a man of a different make *could*), and so he tries to save the child, and loses his life. But he has got what he was after—*his own approval*.

Y. M. What do you call Love, Hate, Charity, Revenge, Humanity, Magnanimity, Forgiveness?

O. M. Different results of the one Master Impulse:

the necessity of securing one's self-approval. They wear diverse clothes and are subject to diverse moods, but in whatsoever ways they masquerade they are the *same person* all the time. To change the figure, the *compulsion* that moves a man—and there is but the one—is the necessity of securing the contentment of his own spirit. When it stops, the man is dead.

Y. M. This is foolishness. Love—

O. M. Why, love is that impulse, that law, in its most uncompromising form. It will squander life and everything else on its object. Not *primarily* for the object's sake, but for *its own.* When its object is happy *it* is happy—and that is what it is unconsciously after.

Y. M. You do not even except the lofty and gracious passion of mother-love?

O. M. No, *it* is the absolute slave of that law. The mother will go naked to clothe her child; she will starve that it may have food; suffer torture to save it from pain; die that it may live. She takes a living *pleasure* in making these sacrifices. *She does it for that reward*—that self-approval, that contentment, that peace, that comfort. *She would do it for your child* IF SHE COULD GET THE SAME PAY.

Y. M. This is an infernal philosophy of yours.

o. m. It is n't a philosophy, it is a fact.

y. m. Of course you must admit that there are some acts which—

o. m. No. There is *no* act, large or small, fine or mean, which springs from any motive but the one— the necessity of appeasing and contenting one's own spirit.

y. m. The world's philanthropists—

o. m. I honor them, I uncover my head to them— from habit and training; but *they* could not know comfort or happiness or self-approval if they did not work and spend for the unfortunate. It makes *them* happy to see others happy; and so with money and labor they buy what they are after—*happiness, self-approval.* Why don't misers do the same thing? Because they can get a thousandfold more happiness by *not* doing it. There is no other reason. They follow the law of their make.

y. m. What do you say of duty for duty's sake?

o. m. That *it does not exist.* Duties are not performed for duty's *sake,* but because their *neglect* would make the man *uncomfortable.* A man performs but *one* duty—the duty of contenting his spirit, the duty of making himself agreeable to himself. If he can most satisfyingly perform this sole and only duty by *helping* his neighbor, he will do it;

if he can most satisfyingly perform it by *swindling* his neighbor, he will do that. But he always looks out for Number One—*first;* the effects upon others are a *secondary* matter. Men pretend to self-sacrifices, but this is a thing which in the ordinary value of the phrase, *does not exist and has not existed.* A man often honestly *thinks* he is sacrificing himself merely and solely for some one else, but he is deceived; his bottom impulse is to content a requirement of his nature and training, and thus acquire peace for his soul.

Y. M. Apparently, then, all men, both good and bad ones, devote their lives to contenting their consciences?

O. M. Yes. That is a good enough name for it: Conscience—that independent Sovereign, that insolent absolute Monarch inside of a man who is the man's Master. There are all kinds of consciences, because there are all kinds of men. You satisfy an assassin's conscience in one way, a philanthropist's in another, a miser's in another, a burglar's in still another. As a *guide* or *incentive* to any authoritatively prescribed line of morals or conduct, (leaving *training* out of the account,) a man's conscience is totally valueless. I knew a kind-hearted Kentuckian whose self-approval was lacking—whose conscience was troubling him, to phrase it with exactness—*because he had neglected to kill a certain man*—a man whom he had never seen. The stranger had killed this man's friend in a fight, this man's Kentucky training made it a duty to kill the stranger for it. He neglected his duty—kept dodging it, shirking it, putting it off, and his unrelenting conscience kept persecuting him for this conduct. At last, to get ease of mind, comfort, self-approval, he hunted up the stranger and took his life. It was an immense act of *self-sacrifice*, (as per the usual definition,) for he did not want to do it, and he never would have done it if he could have bought a contented spirit and an unworried mind at smaller cost. But we are so made that we will pay *anything* for that contentment—even another man's life.

Y. M. You spoke a moment ago of *trained* consciences. You mean that we are not *born* with consciences competent to guide us aright?

O. M. If we were, children and savages would know right from wrong, and not have to be taught it.

Y. M. But consciences can be *trained?*

O. M. Yes.

Y. M. Of course by parents, teachers, the pulpit, and books.

o. m. Yes—they do their share; they do what they can.

y. m. And the rest is done by—

o. m. Oh, a million unnoticed influences—for good or bad: influences which work without rest during every waking moment of a man's life, from cradle to grave.

y. m. You have tabulated these?

o. m. Many of them—yes.

y. m. Will you read me the result?

o. m. Another time, yes. It would take an hour.

y. m. A conscience can be trained to shun evil and prefer good?

o. m. Yes.

y. m. But will prefer it for spirit-contenting reasons only?

o. m. It *can't* be trained to do a thing for any *other* reason. The thing is impossible.

y. m. There *must* be a genuinely and utterly self-sacrificing act recorded in human history somewhere.

o. m. You are young. You have many years before you. Search one out.

y. m. It does seem to me that when a man sees a fellow-being struggling in the water and jumps in at the risk of his life to save him—

O. M. Wait. Describe the *man*. Describe the *fellow-being*. State if there is an *audience* present; or if they are *alone*.

Y. M. What have these things to do with the splendid act?

O. M. Very much. Shall we suppose, as a beginning, that the two are alone, in a solitary place, at midnight?

Y. M. If you choose.

O. M. And that the fellow-being is the man's daughter?

Y. M. Well, n—no—make it some one else.

O. M. A filthy, drunken ruffian, then?

Y. M. I see. Circumstances alter cases. I suppose that if there was no audience to observe the act, the man would n't perform it.

O. M. But there is here and there a man who *would*. People, for instance, like the man who lost his life trying to save the child from the fire; and the man who gave the needy old woman his 25 cents and walked home in the storm—there are here and there men like that who would do it. And why? Because they could n't *bear* to see a fellow-being struggling in the water and not jump in and help. It would give *them* pain. They would save the fellow-being on that account. *They would n't do it otherwise.*

They strictly obey the law which I have been insisting upon. You must remember and always distinguish the people who *can't bear* things from the people who *can*. It will throw light upon a number of apparently "self-sacrificing" cases.

Y. M. Oh, dear, it 's all so disgusting.

O. M. Yes. And so true.

Y. M. Come—take the good boy who does things he does n't want to do, in order to gratify his mother.

O. M. He does seven-tenths of the act because it gratifies *him* to gratify his mother. Throw the bulk of advantage the other way and the good boy would not do the act. He *must* obey the iron law. None can escape it.

Y. M. Well, take the case of a bad boy who—

O. M. You need n't mention it, it is a waste of time. It is no matter about the bad boy's act. Whatever it was, he had a spirit-contenting reason for it. Otherwise you have been misinformed, and he did n't do it.

Y. M. It is very exasperating. A while ago you said that a man's conscience is not a born judge of morals and conduct, but has to be taught and trained. Now I think a conscience can get drowsy and lazy, but I don't think it can go wrong; and if you wake it up—

A LITTLE STORY

O. M. I will tell you a little story:

Once upon a time an Infidel was guest in the house of a Christian widow whose little boy was ill and near to death. The Infidel often watched by the bedside and entertained the boy with talk, and he used these opportunities to satisfy a strong longing of his nature—that desire which is in us all to better other people's condition by having them think as we think. He was successful. But the dying boy, in his last moments, reproached him and said—

"I believed, and was happy in it; you have taken my belief away, and my comfort. Now I have nothing left, and I die miserable; for the things which you have told me do not take the place of that which I have lost."

And the mother, also, reproached the Infidel, and said—

"My child is forever lost, and my heart is broken. How could you do this cruel thing? We have done you no harm, but only kindness; we made our house your home, you were welcome to all we had, and this is our reward."

The heart of the Infidel was filled with remorse for what he had done, and he said:

"It was wrong—I see it now: but I was only try-ing to do him good. In my view he was in error; it seemed my duty to teach him the truth."

Then the mother said—

"I had taught him, all his little life, what I be-lieved to be the truth, and in his believing faith both of us were happy. Now he is dead—and lost; and I am miserable. Our faith came down to us through centuries of believing ancestors; what right had you, or any one, to disturb it? Where was your honor, where was your shame?"

Y. M. He was a miscreant, and deserved death!

O. M. He thought so himself, and said so.

Y. M. Ah—you see, *his conscience was awakened!*

O. M. Yes—his Self-Disapproval was. It *pained* him to see the mother suffer. He was sorry he had done a thing which brought *him* pain. It did not occur to him to think of the mother when he was mis-teaching the boy, for he was absorbed in provid-ing *pleasure* for himself, then. Providing it by sat-isfying what he believed to be a call of duty.

Y. M. Call it what you please, it is to me a case of *awakened conscience*. That awakened conscience could never get itself into that species of trouble again. A cure like that is a *permanent* cure.

O. M. Pardon—I had not finished the story. We

are creatures of *outside influences*—we originate *nothing* within. Whenever we take a new line of thought and drift into a new line of belief and action, the impulse is *always* suggested from the *outside.* Remorse so preyed upon the Infidel that it dissolved his harshness toward the boy's religion and made him come to regard it with tolerance, next with kindness, for the boy's sake and the mother's. Finally he found himself examining it. From that moment his progress in his new trend was steady and rapid. He became a believing Christian. And now his remorse for having robbed the dying boy of his faith and his salvation was bitterer than ever. It gave him no rest, no peace. He *must* have rest and peace—it is the law of our nature. There seemed but one way to get it; he must devote himself to saving imperiled souls. He became a missionary. He landed in a pagan country ill and helpless. A native widow took him into her humble home and nursed him back to convalescence. Then her young boy was taken hopelessly ill, and the grateful missionary helped her tend him. Here was his first opportunity to repair a part of the wrong done to the other boy by doing a precious service for this one by undermining his foolish faith in his false gods. He was successful.

But the dying boy in his last moments reproached him and said—

"I believed, and was happy in it; you have taken my belief away, and my comfort. Now I have nothing left, and I die miserable; for the things which you have told me do not take the place of that which I have lost."

And the mother, also, reproached the missionary, and said—

"My child is forever lost, and my heart is broken. How could you do this cruel thing? We had done you no harm, but only kindness; we made our house your home, you were welcome to all we had, and this is our reward."

The heart of the missionary was filled with remorse for what he had done, and he said—

"It was wrong—I see it now; but I was only trying to do him good. In my view he was in error; it seemed my duty to teach him the truth."

Then the mother said—

"I had taught him, all his little life, what I believed to be the truth, and in his believing faith both of us were happy. Now he is dead—and lost; and I am miserable. Our faith came down to us through centuries of believing ancestors; what right had you,

*or any one, to disturb it?   Where was your honor,
where was your shame?"*

The missionary's anguish of remorse and sense of
treachery were as bitter and persecuting and unap-
peasable, now, as they had been in the former case.
The story is finished.   What is your comment?

Y. M. The man's conscience was a fool!   It was
morbid.   It did n't know right from wrong.

O. M. I am not sorry to hear you say that.   If you
grant that *one* man's conscience does n't know right
from wrong, it is an admission that there are others
like it.   This single admission pulls down the whole
doctrine of infallibility of judgment in consciences.
Meantime there is one thing which I ask you to
notice.

Y. M. What is that?

O. M. That in both cases the man's *act* gave him
no spiritual discomfort, and that he was quite satisfied with it and got pleasure out of it.   But afterward when it resulted in *pain to him,* he was sorry.
Sorry it had inflicted pain upon the others, *but for
no reason under the sun except that their pain gave
HIM pain..* Our consciences take *no* notice of pain
inflicted upon others until it reaches a point where
it gives pain to *us.*   In *all* cases without exception we
are absolutely indifferent to another person's pain

until his sufferings make us uncomfortable. Many an infidel would not have been troubled by that Christian mother's distress. Don't you believe that?

Y. M. Yes. You might almost say it of the *average* infidel, I think.

O. M. And many a missionary, sternly fortified by his sense of duty, would not have been troubled by the pagan mother's distress—Jesuit missionaries in Canada in the early French times, for instance; see episodes quoted by Parkman.

Y. M. Well, let us adjourn. Where have we arrived?

O. M. At this. That we (mankind) have ticketed ourselves with a number of qualities to which we have given misleading names. Love, Hate, Charity, Compassion, Avarice, Benevolence, and so on. I mean we attach misleading *meanings* to the names. They are all forms of self-contentment, self-gratification, but the names so disguise them that they distract our attention from the fact. Also we have smuggled a word into the dictionary which ought not to be there at all—Self-Sacrifice. It describes a thing which does not exist. But worst of all, we ignore and never mention the Sole Impulse which dictates and compels a man's every act: the imperious necessity of securing his own approval, in every emergency and at all costs.   To it we owe all that we are.   It is our breath, our heart, our blood.   It is our only spur, our whip, our goad, our only impelling power; we have no other.   Without it we should be mere inert images, corpses; no one would do anything, there would be no progress, the world would stand still.   We ought to stand reverently uncovered when the name of that stupendous power is uttered.

Y. M. I am not convinced.

O. M. You will be when you think.

III

Instances in Point

O. M. Have you given thought to the Gospel of Self-Approval since we talked?

Y. M. I have.

O. M. It was I that moved you to it. That is to say an *outside influence* moved you to it—not one that originated in your own head. Will you try to keep that in mind and not forget it?

Y. M. Yes. Why?

O. M. Because by and by in one of our talks, I wish to further impress upon you that neither you, nor I, nor any man ever originates a thought in his own head. *The utterer of a thought always utters a second-hand one.*

Y. M. Oh, now—

O. M. Wait. Reserve your remark till we get to that part of our discussion—to-morrow or next day, say. Now, then, have you been considering the proposition that no act is ever born of any but a self-contenting impulse—(primarily). You have sought. What have you found?

Y. M. I have not been very fortunate. I have examined many fine and apparently self-sacrificing deeds in romances and biographies, but—

O. M. Under searching analysis the ostensible self-sacrifice disappeared? It naturally would.

Y. M. But here in this novel is one which seems to promise. In the Adirondack woods is a wage-earner and lay preacher in the lumber-camps who is of noble character and deeply religious. An earnest and practical laborer in the New York slums comes up there on vacation—he is leader of a section of the University Settlement. Holme, the lumberman, is fired with a desire to throw away his excellent worldly prospects and go down and save souls on the East Side. He counts it happiness to make this sacrifice for the glory of God and for the cause of Christ. He resigns his place, makes the sacrifice cheerfully, and goes to the East Side and preaches Christ and Him crucified every day and every night to little groups of half-civilized foreign paupers who scoff at him. But he rejoices in the scoffings, since he is suffering them in the great cause of Christ. You have so filled my mind with suspicions that I was constantly expecting to find a hidden questionable impulse back of all this, but I am thankful to say I have failed. This man saw his duty, and for *duty's sake* he sacrificed self and assumed the burden it imposed.

o. m. Is that as far as you have read?

y. m. Yes.

o. m. Let us read further, presently. Meantime, in sacrificing himself—*not* for the glory of God, *primarily*, as *he* imagined, but *first* to content that exacting and inflexible master within him—*did he sacrifice anybody else?*

y. m. How do you mean?

o. m. He relinquished a lucrative post and got mere food and lodging in place of it. Had he dependants?

y. m. Well—yes.

o. m. In what way and to what extent did his self-sacrifice affect *them?*

y. m. He was the support of a superannuated father. He had a young sister with a remarkable voice—he was giving her a musical education, so that her longing to be self-supporting might be gratified. He was furnishing the money to put a young brother through a polytechnic school and satisfy his desire to become a civil engineer.

O. M. The old father's comforts were now curtailed?

Y. M. Quite seriously. Yes.

O. M. The sister's music-lessons had to stop?

Y. M. Yes.

O. M. The young brother's education—well, an extinguishing blight fell upon that happy dream, and he had to go to sawing wood to support the old father, or something like that?

Y. M. It is about what happened. Yes.

O. M. What a handsome job of self-sacrificing he did do! It seems to me that he sacrificed everybody *except* himself. Have n't I told you that no man *ever* sacrifices himself; that there is no instance of it upon record anywhere; and that when a man's Interior Monarch requires a thing of its slave for either its *momentary* or its *permanent* contentment, that thing must and will be furnished and that command obeyed, no matter who may stand in the way and suffer disaster by it? That man *ruined his family* to please and content his Interior Monarch—

Y. M. And help Christ's cause.

O. M. Yes—*secondly*. Not firstly. *He* thought it was firstly.

Y. M. Very well, have it so, if you will. But it

could be that he argued that if he saved a hundred souls in New York—

O. M. The sacrifice of the *family* would be justified by that great profit upon the—the—what shall we call it?

Y. M. Investment?

O. M. Hardly. How would *speculation* do? how would *gamble* do? Not a solitary soul-capture was sure. He played for a possible thirty-three hundred per cent profit. It was *gambling*—with his family for "chips." However, let us see how the game came out. Maybe we can get on the track of the secret original impulse, the *real* impulse, that moved him to so nobly self-sacrifice his family in the Savior's cause under the superstition that he was sacrificing himself. I will read a chapter or so...... Here we have it! it was bound to expose itself sooner or later. He preached to the East-Side rabble a season, then went back to his old dull, obscure life in the lumber camps *"hurt to the heart, his pride humbled."* Why? Were not his efforts acceptable to the Savior, for Whom alone they were made? Dear me, that detail is *lost sight of*, is not even referred to, the fact that it started out as a motive is entirely forgotten! Then what is the trouble? The authoress quite innocently and unconsciously gives the whole business away. The trouble was this: this man merely *preached* to the poor; that is not the University Settlement's way; it deals in larger and better things than that, and it did not enthuse over that crude Salvation-Army eloquence. It was courteous to Holme—but cool. It did not pet him, did not take him to its bosom. *"Perished were all his dreams of distinction, the praise and grateful approval of—"* Of whom? The Savior? No; the Savior is not mentioned. Of whom, then? Of " his *fellow-workers.*" Why did he want that? Because the Master inside of him wanted it, and would not be content without it. That emphasized sentence quoted above, reveals the secret we have been seeking, the original impulse, the *real* impulse, which moved the obscure and unappreciated Adirondack lumberman to sacrifice his family and go on that crusade to the East-Side—which said original impulse was this, to-wit: without knowing it *he went there to show a neglectful world the large talent that was in him, and rise to distinction.* As I have warned you before, *no* act springs from any but the one law, the one motive. But I pray you, do not accept this law upon my say-so; but diligently examine for yourself. Whenever you read of a self-sacrificing act or hear of one, or of a duty done for *duty's sake*, take it to pieces and look for the *real* motive. It is always there.

Y. M. I do it every day. I cannot help it, now that I have gotten started upon the degrading and exasperating quest. For it is hatefully interesting! — in fact, fascinating is the word. As soon as I come across a golden deed in a book I have to stop and take it apart and examine it, I cannot help myself.

O. M. Have you ever found one that defeated the rule?

Y. M. No—at least, not yet. But take the case of servant-tipping in Europe. You pay the *hotel* for service; you owe the servants *nothing*, yet you pay them besides. Does n't that defeat it?

O. M. In what way?

Y. M. You are not *obliged* to do it, therefore its source is compassion for their ill-paid condition, and—

O. M. Has that custom ever vexed you, annoyed you, irritated you?

Y. M. Well—yes.

O. M. Still you succumbed to it?

Y. M. Of course.

O. M. Why of course?

Y. M. Well, custom is law, in a way, and laws

must be submitted to—everybody recognizes it as a *duty*.

O. M. Then you pay the irritating tax for *duty's* sake?

Y. M. I suppose it amounts to that.

O. M. Then the impulse which moves you to submit to the tax is not *all* compassion, charity, benevolence?

Y. M. Well—perhaps not.

O. M. Is *any* of it?

Y. M. I—perhaps I was too hasty in locating its source.

O. M. Perhaps so. In case you ignored the custom would you get prompt and effective service from the servants?

Y. M. Oh, hear yourself talk! Those European servants? Why, you would n't get any at all, to speak of.

O. M. Could n't *that* work as an impulse to move you to pay the tax?

Y. M. I am not denying it.

O. M. Apparently, then, it is a case of for-duty's-sake with a little self-interest added?

Y. M. Yes, it has the look of it. But here is a point: we pay that tax knowing it to be unjust and

an extortion; yet we go away with a pain at the
heart if we think we have been stingy with the poor
fellows; and we heartily wish we were back again,
so that we could do the right thing, and *more* than
the right thing, the *generous* thing. I think it will be
difficult for you to find any thought of self in that
impulse.

o. m. I wonder why you should think so. When
you find service charged in the *hotel* bill does it an-
noy you?

y. m. No.

o. m. Do you ever complain of the amount of it?

y. m. No, it would not occur to me.

o. m. The *expense,* then, is not the annoying detail. It is a fixed charge, and you pay it cheerfully,
you pay it without a murmur. When you came to
pay the servants, how would you like it if each of the
men and maids had a fixed charge?

y. m. Like it? I should rejoice!

o. m. Even if the fixed tax were a shade *more*
than you had been in the habit of paying in the form
of tips?

y. m. Indeed, yes!

o. m. Very well, then. As I understand it, it is n't
really compassion nor yet duty that moves you to

pay the tax, and it is n't the *amount* of the tax that annoys you. Yet *something* annoys you. What is it?

Y. M. Well, the trouble is, you never know *what* to pay, the tax varies so, all over Europe.

O. M. So you have to guess?

Y. M. There is no other way. So you go on thinking and thinking, and calculating and guessing, and consulting with other people and getting their views; and it spoils your sleep nights, and makes you distraught in the day-time, and while you are pretending to look at the sights you are only guessing and guessing and guessing all the time, and being worried and miserable.

O. M. And all about a debt which you don't owe and don't have to pay unless you want to! Strange. What is the purpose of the guessing?

Y. M. To guess out what is right to give them, and not be unfair to any of them.

O. M. It has quite a noble look—taking so much pains and using up so much valuable time in order to be just and fair to a poor servant to whom you owe nothing, but who needs money and is ill paid.

Y. M. I think, myself, that if there is any ungracious motive back of it it will be hard to find.

O. M. How do you know when you have not paid a servant fairly?

Y. M. Why, he is silent; does not thank you. Sometimes he gives you a look that makes you ashamed. You are too proud to rectify your mistake there, with people looking, but afterward you keep on wishing and wishing you *had* done it. My, the shame and the pain of it! Sometimes you see, by the signs, that you have hit it *just right,* and you go away mightily satisfied. Sometimes the man is so effusively thankful that you know you have given him a good deal *more* than was necessary.

O. M. *Necessary?* Necessary for what?

Y. M. To content him.

O. M. How do you feel *then?*

Y. M. Repentant.

O. M. It is my belief that you have *not* been concerning yourself in guessing out his just dues, but only in ciphering out what would *content* him. And I think you had a self-deluding reason for that.

Y. M. What was it?

O. M. If you fell short of what he was expecting and wanting, you would get a look which would *shame you before folk.* That would give you *pain.* *You*—for you are only working for yourself, not *him.* If you gave him too much you would be *ashamed of yourself* for it, and that would give *you* pain—another case of thinking of *yourself,* protecting yourself, *saving yourself from discomfort.* You never think of the servant once—except to guess out how to get *his approval*. If you get that, you get your *own* approval, and that is the sole and only thing you are after. The Master inside of you is then satisfied, contented, comfortable; there was *no other* thing at stake, as a matter of *first* interest, anywhere in the transaction.

FURTHER INSTANCES

Y. M. Well, to think of it: Self-Sacrifice for others, the grandest thing in man, ruled out! non-existent!

O. M. Are you accusing me of saying that?

Y. M. Why, certainly.

O. M. I have n't said it.

Y. M. What did you say, then?

O. M. That no man has ever sacrificed himself in the common meaning of that phrase—which is, self-sacrifice for another *alone*. Men make daily sacrifices for others, but it is for their own sake *first*. The act must content their own spirit *first*. The other beneficiaries come second.

Y. M. And the same with duty for duty's sake?

O. M. Yes. No man performs a duty for mere duty's sake; the act must content his spirit *first*. He must feel better for *doing* the duty than he would for shirking it.   Otherwise he will not do it.

Y. M. Take the case of the *Berkeley Castle*.

O. M. It was a noble duty, greatly performed. Take it to pieces and examine it, if you like.

Y. M. A British troop-ship crowded with soldiers and their wives and children.   She struck a rock and began to sink.   There was room in the boats for the women and children only.   The colonel lined-up his regiment on the deck and said "it is our duty to die, that they may be saved."   There was no murmur, no protest.   The boats carried away the women and children.   When the death-moment was come, the colonel and his officers took their several posts, the men stood at shoulder-arms, and so, as on dress-parade, with their flag flying and the drums beating, they went down, a sacrifice to duty for duty's sake. Can you view it as other than that?

O. M. It was something as fine as that, as exalted as that.   Could you have remained in those ranks and gone down to your death in that unflinching way?

Y. M. Could I?   No, I could not.

O. M. Think.   Imagine yourself there, with that watery doom creeping higher and higher around you.

Y. M. I can imagine it.   I feel all the horror of it.

I could not have endured it, I could not have remained in my place. I know it.

O. M. Why?

Y. M. There is no why about it: I know myself, and I know I could n't *do* it.

O. M. But it would be your *duty* to do it.

Y. M. Yes, I know—but I could n't.

O. M. It was more than a thousand men, yet not one of them flinched. Some of them must have been born with your temperament; if they could do that great duty for duty's *sake*, why not you? Don't you know that you could go out and gather together a thousand clerks and mechanics and put them on that deck and ask them to die for duty's sake, and not two dozen of them would stay in the ranks to the end?

Y. M. Yes, I know that.

O. M. But you *train* them, and put them through a campaign or two; then they would be soldiers; soldiers, with a soldier's pride, a soldier's self-respect, a soldier's ideals. They would have to content a *soldier's* spirit then, not a clerk's, not a mechanic's. They could not content that spirit by shirking a soldier's duty, could they?

Y. M. I suppose not.

O. M. Then they would do the duty not for the

duty's sake, but for their *own* sake—primarily. The *duty* was *just the same*, and just as imperative, when they were clerks, mechanics, raw recruits, but they would n't perform it for that. As clerks and mechanics they had other ideals, another spirit to satisfy, and they satisfied it. They *had* to; it is the law. *Training* is potent. Training toward higher and higher, and ever higher ideals is worth any man's thought and labor and diligence.

Y. M. Consider the man who stands by his duty and goes to the stake rather than be recreant to it.

O. M. It is his make and his training. He has to content the spirit that is in him, though it cost him his life. Another man, just as sincerely religious, but of different temperament, will fail of that duty, though recognizing it as a duty, and grieving to be unequal to it: but he must content the spirit that is in him—he cannot help it. He could not perform that duty for duty's *sake*, for that would not content his spirit, and the contenting of his spirit must be looked to *first*. It takes precedence of all other duties.

Y. M. Take the case of a clergyman of stainless private morals who votes for a thief for public office, on his own party's ticket, and against an honest man on the other ticket.

o. M. He has to content his spirit. He has no public morals: he has no private ones, where his party's prosperity is at stake. He will always be true to his make and training.

TRAINING

IV

Training

Y. M. You keep using that word—training. By it do you particularly mean—

O. M. Study, instruction, lectures, sermons? That is a part of it—but not a large part. I mean *all* the outside influences. There are a million of them. From the cradle to the grave, during all his waking hours, the human being is under training. In the very first rank of his trainers stands *association*. It is his human environment which influences his mind and his feelings, furnishes him his ideals, and sets him on his road and keeps him in it. If he leave that road he will find himself shunned by the people whom he most loves and esteems, and whose approval he most values. He is a chameleon; by the law of his nature he takes the color of his place of resort. The influences about him create his preferences, his aversions, his politics, his tastes, his morals, his religion. He creates none of these things for himself. He *thinks* he does, but that is because he has not examined into the matter. You have seen Presbyterians?

Y. M. Many.

O. M. How did they happen to be Presbyterians and not Congregationalists? And why were the Congregationalists not Baptists, and the Baptists Roman Catholics, and the Roman Catholics Buddhists, and the Buddhists Quakers, and the Quakers Episcopalians, and the Episcopalians Millerites, and the Millerites Hindoos, and the Hindoos Atheists, and the Atheists Spiritualists, and the Spiritualists Agnostics, and the Agnostics Methodists, and the Methodists Confucians, and the Confucians Unitarians, and the Unitarians Mohammedans, and the Mohammedans Salvation Warriors, and the Salvation Warriors Zoroastrians, and the Zoroastrians Christian Scientists, and the Christian Scientists Mormons—and so on?

Y. M. You may answer your question yourself.

O. M. That list of sects is not a record of *studies*, searchings, seekings after light; it mainly (and sarcastically) indicates what *association* can do. If you know a man's nationality you can come within a split hair of guessing the complexion of his religion: English—Protestant; American—ditto; Spaniard, Frenchman, Irishman, Italian, South American, Austrian—Roman Catholic; Russian—Greek Catholic; Turk—Mohammedan; and so on. And when you know the man's religious complexion, you know what sort of religious books he reads when he wants some more light, and what sort of books he avoids, lest by accident he get more light than he wants. In America if you know which party-collar a voter wears, you know what his associations are, and how he came by his politics, and which breed of newspaper he reads to get light, and which breed he diligently avoids, and which breed of mass meetings he attends in order to broaden his political knowledge, and which breed of mass meetings he does n't attend, except to refute its doctrines with brickbats. We are always hearing of people who are around *seeking after Truth.* I have never seen a (permanent) specimen. I think he has never lived. But I have seen several entirely sincere people who *thought* they were (permanent) Seekers after Truth. They sought diligently, persistently, carefully, cautiously, profoundly, with perfect honesty and nicely adjusted judgment—until they believed that without doubt or question they had found the Truth. *That was the end of the search.* The man spent the rest of his life hunting up shingles wherewith to protect his Truth from the weather. If he was seeking after political Truth he found it in one or another of the hundred political gospels which govern men in the

earth; if he was seeking after the Only True Religion he found it in one or another of the three thous-
and that are on the market. In any case, when he
found the Truth *he sought no further;* but from that
day forth, with his soldering iron in one hand and
his bludgeon in the other he tinkered its leaks and
reasoned with objectors. There have been innumer-
able Temporary Seekers after Truth—have you ever
heard of a permanent one? In the very nature of
man such a person is impossible. However, to drop
back to the text—training: all training is one form
or another of *outside influence,* and *association* is
the largest part of it. A man is never anything but
what his outside influences have made him. They
train him downwards or they train him upwards—
but they *train* him; they are at work upon him all the
time.

Y. M. Then if he happen by the accidents of life
to be evilly placed there is no help for him, according
to your notions—he must train downwards.

O. M. No help for him? No help for this chameleon? It is a mistake. It is in his chameleonship
that his greatest good fortune lies. He has only to
change his habitat—his *associations.* But the impulse to do it must come from the *outside*—he cannot originate it himself, with that purpose in view.

Sometimes a very small and accidental thing can furnish him the initiatory impulse and start him on a new road, with a new ideal. The chance remark of a sweetheart, "I hear that you are a coward" may water a seed that shall sprout and bloom and flourish, and end in producing a surprising fruitage—in the fields of war. The history of man is full of such accidents. The accident of a broken leg brought a profane and ribald soldier under religious influences and furnished him a new ideal. From that accident sprang the Order of the Jesuits, and it has been shaking thrones, changing policies, and doing other tremendous work for two hundred years—and will go on. The chance reading of a book, or of a paragraph in a newspaper can start a man on a new track and make him renounce his old associations and seek new ones that are *in sympathy with his new ideal*: and the result, for that man, can be an entire change of his way of life.

Y. M. Are you hinting at a scheme of procedure?

O. M. Not a new one—an old one. Old as mankind.

Y. M. What is it?

O. M. Merely the laying of traps for people. Traps baited with *Initiatory Impulses toward high ideals*. It is what the tract distributor does. It is

what the missionary does. It is what governments
ought to do.

Y. M. Don't they?

O. M. In one way they do, in another way they
don't. They separate the small-pox patients from the
healthy people, but in dealing with crime they put
the healthy into the pest-house along with the
sick. That is to say, they put the beginners in with
the confirmed criminals. This would be well if man
were naturally inclined to good, but he is n't, and so
association makes the beginners worse than they
were when they went into captivity. It is putting a
very severe punishment upon the comparatively innocent. However, all governments are hard on the
innocent at times. They hang a man—which is a trifling punishment; this breaks the hearts of his family
—which is a heavy one. They comfortably jail and
feed a wife-beater, and leave his innocent wife and
children to starve.

Y. M. Do you believe in the doctrine that man is
equipped with an intuitive perception of good and
evil?

O. M. Adam had n't it.

Y. M. But has man acquired it since?

O. M. No. I think he has no intuitions of any
kind. He gets *all* his ideas, all his impressions, from

the outside. I keep repeating this, in the hope that I may so impress it upon you that you will be interested to observe and examine for yourself and see whether it is true or false.

Y. M. Where did you get your own aggravating notions?

O. M. From the *outside.* I did not invent them. They are gathered from a thousand unknown sources. Mainly *unconsciously* gathered.

Y. M. Don't you believe that God could make an inherently honest man?

O. M. Yes, I know He could. I also know that He never did make one.

Y. M. A wiser observer than you has recorded the fact that "an honest man 's the noblest work of God."

O. M. He did n't record a fact, he recorded a falsity. It is windy, and sounds well, but it is not true. God makes a man with honest and dishonest *possibilities* in him and stops there. The man's *associations* develop the possibilities—the one set or the other. The result is accordingly an honest man or a dishonest one.

Y. M. And the honest one is not entitled to—

O. M. Praise? No. How often must I tell you that? *He* is not the architect of his honesty.

Y. M. Now then, I will ask you where there is any sense in training people to lead virtuous lives. What is gained by it?

O. M. The man himself gets large advantages out of it, and that is the main thing—to *him*. He is not a peril to his neighbors, he is not a damage to them —and so *they* get an advantage out of his virtues. That is the main thing to *them*. It can make this life comparatively comfortable to the parties concerned; the *neglect* of this training can make this life a constant peril and distress to the parties concerned.

Y. M. You have said that training is everything; that training is the man *himself*, for it makes him what he is.

O. M. I said training and *another* thing. Let that other thing pass, for the moment. What were you going to say?

Y. M. We have an old servant. She has been with us twenty-two years. Her service used to be faultless, but now she has become very forgetful. We are all fond of her; we all recognize that she cannot help the infirmity which age has brought her; the rest of the family do not scold her for her remissnesses, but at times I do—I can't seem to control myself. Don't I try? I do try. Now, then, when I was ready to dress, this morning, no clean clothes had been put out. I lost my temper; I lose it easiest and quickest in the early morning. I rang; and immediately began to warn myself not to show temper, and to be careful and speak gently. I safeguarded myself most carefully. I even chose the very words I would use: "You 've forgotten the clean clothes, Jane." When she appeared in the door I opened my mouth to say that phrase—and out of it, moved by an instant surge of passion which I was not expecting and had n't time to put under control, came the hot rebuke, "You 've forgotten them again!" You say a man always does the thing which will best please his Interior Master. Whence came the impulse to make careful preparation to save the girl the humiliation of a rebuke? Did that come from the Master, who is always primarily concerned about *himself?*

O. M. Unquestionably. There is no other source for any impulse. *Secondarily* you made preparation to save the girl, but *primarily* its object was to save yourself, by contenting the Master.

Y. M. How do you mean?

O. M. Has any member of the family ever implored you to watch your temper and not fly out at the girl?

Y. M. Yes. My mother.

O. M. You love her?

Y. M. Oh, more than that!

O. M. You would always do anything in your power to please her?

Y. M. It is a delight to me to do anything to please her!

O. M. Why? *You would do it for pay, solely—* for *profit.* What profit would you expect and certainly receive from the investment?

Y. M. Personally? None. To please *her* is enough.

O. M. It appears, then, that your object, primarily, *was n't* to save the girl a humiliation, but to *please your mother.* It also appears that to please your mother gives *you* a strong pleasure. Is not that the profit which you get out of the investment? Is n't that the *real* profit and *first* profit?

Y. M. Oh, well? Go on.

O. M. In *all* transactions, the Interior Master looks to it that *you get the first profit.* Otherwise there is no transaction.

Y. M. Well, then, if I was so anxious to get that profit and so intent upon it, why did I throw it away by losing my temper?

O. M. In order to get *another* profit which suddenly superseded it in value.

Y. M. Where was it?

O. M. Ambushed behind your born temperament,

and waiting for a chance. Your native warm temper suddenly jumped to the front, and *for the moment* its influence was more powerful than your mother's, and abolished it. In that instance you were eager to flash out a hot rebuke and enjoy it. You did enjoy it, did n't you?

Y. M. For—for a quarter of a second. Yes—I did.

O. M. Very well, it is as I have said: the thing which will give you the *most* pleasure, the most satisfaction, in any moment or *fraction* of a moment, is the thing you will always do. You must content the Master's *latest* whim, whatever it may be.

Y. M. But when the tears came into the old servant's eyes I could have cut my hand off for what I had done.

O. M. Right. You had humiliated *yourself*, you see, you had given yourself *pain*. Nothing is of *first* importance to a man except results which damage *him* or profit him—all the rest is *secondary*. Your Master was displeased with you, although you had obeyed him. He required a prompt *repentance;* you obeyed again; you *had* to—there is never any escape from his commands. He is a hard master and fickle; he changes his mind in the fraction of a second, but you must be ready to obey, and you will obey, *always*. If he requires repentance, to content him, you will always furnish it. He must be nursed, petted, coddled, and kept contented, let the terms be what they may.

Y. M. Training! Oh, what is the use of it? Did n't I, and did n't my mother try to train me up to where I would no longer fly out at that girl?

O. M. Have you never managed to keep back a scolding?

Y. M. Oh, certainly—many times.

O. M. More times this year than last?

Y. M. Yes, a good many more.

O. M. More times last year than the year before?

Y. M. Yes.

O. M. There is a large improvement, then, in the two years?

Y. M. Yes, undoubtedly.

O. M. Then your question is answered. You see there *is* use in training. Keep on. Keep faithfully on. You are doing well.

Y. M. Will my reform reach perfection?

O. M. It will. Up to *your* limit.

Y. M. My limit? What do you mean by that?

O. M. You remember that you said that I said training was *everything*. I corrected you, and said "training and *another* thing." That other thing is *temperament*—that is, the disposition you were born with. *You can't eradicate your disposition nor any rag of it*—you can only put a pressure on it and keep it down and quiet. You have a warm temper?

Y. M. Yes.

O. M. You will never get rid of it; but by watching it you can keep it down nearly all the time. *Its presence is your limit.* Your reform will never quite reach perfection, for your temper will beat you now and then, but you will come near enough. You have made valuable progress and can make more. There *is* use in training. Immense use. Presently you will reach a new stage of development, then your progress will be easier; will proceed on a simpler basis, anyway.

Y. M. Explain.

O. M. You keep back your scoldings now, to please *yourself* by pleasing your *mother*; presently the mere triumphing over your temper will delight your vanity and confer a more delicious pleasure and satisfaction upon you than even the approbation of your *mother* confers upon you now. You will then labor for yourself directly and at *first hands*, not by the roundabout way through your mother. It simplifies the matter, and it also strengthens the impulse.

Y. M. Ah, dear! But I shan't ever reach the point

where I will spare the girl for *her* sake *primarily*, not mine?

O. M. Why—yes. In heaven.

Y. M. (*After a reflective pause.*) Temperament. Well, I see one must allow for temperament. It is a large factor, sure enough. My mother is thoughtful, and not hot-tempered. When I was dressed I went to her room; she was not there; I called, she answered from the bath-room. I heard the water running. I inquired. She answered, without temper, that Jane had forgotten her bath, and she was preparing it herself. I offered to ring, but she said, "No, don't do that; it would only distress her to be confronted with her lapse, and would be a rebuke; she does n't deserve that—she is not to blame for the tricks her memory serves her." I say—has my mother an Interior Master?—and where was he?

O. M. He was there. There, and looking out for his own peace and pleasure and contentment. The girl's distress would have pained *your mother*. Otherwise the girl would have been rung up, distress and all. I know women who would have gotten a No. 1 *pleasure* out of ringing Jane up—and so they would infallibly have pushed the button and obeyed the law of their make and training, which are the servants of their Interior Masters. It is quite likely that a part of your mother's forbearance came from train-ing. The *good* kind of training—whose best and highest function is to see to it that every time it con-fers a satisfaction upon its pupil a benefit shall fall at second hand upon others.

Y. M. If you were going to condense into an ad-monition your plan for the general betterment of the race's condition, how would you word it?

ADMONITION

O. M. Diligently train your ideals *upward* and *still upward* toward a summit where you will find your chiefest pleasure in conduct which, while contenting you, will be sure to confer benefits upon your neigh-bor and the community.

Y. M. Is that a new gospel?

O. M. No.

Y. M. It has been taught before?

O. M. For ten thousand years.

Y. M. By whom?

O. M. All the great religions—all the great gospels.

Y. M. Then there is nothing new about it?

O. M. Oh, yes, there is. It is candidly stated, this time. That has not been done before.

Y. M. How do you mean?

O. M. Have n't I put *you* FIRST, and your neighbor and the community *afterward?*

Y. M. Well, yes, that is a difference, it is true.

O. M. The difference between straight speaking and crooked; the difference between frankness and shuffling.

Y. M. Explain.

O. M. The others offer you a hundred bribes to be good, thus conceding that the Master inside of you must be conciliated and contented first, and that you will do nothing at *first-hand* but for his sake; then they turn square around and require you to do good for *others'* sake *chiefly;* and to do your duty for duty's *sake,* chiefly; and to do acts of *self-sacrifice.* Thus at the outset we all stand upon the same ground —recognition of the supreme and absolute Monarch that resides in man, and we all grovel before him and appeal to him; then those others dodge and shuffle, and face around and unfrankly and inconsistently and illogically change the form of their appeal and direct its persuasions to man's *second-place* powers and to powers which have *no existence* in him, thus advancing them to *first* place; whereas in my Admonition I stick logically and consistently to the original position: I place the Interior Master's requirements *first*, and keep them there.

Y. M. If we grant, for the sake of argument, that your scheme and the other schemes aim at and produce the same result—*right living*—has yours an advantage over the others?

O. M. One, yes—a large one. It has no concealments, no deceptions. When a man leads a right and valuable life under it he is not deceived as to the *real* chief motive which impels him to it—in those other cases he is.

Y. M. Is that an advantage? Is it an advantage to live a lofty life for a mean reason? In the other cases he lives the lofty life under the *impression* that he is living it for a lofty reason. Is not that an advantage?

O. M. Perhaps so. The same advantage he might get out of thinking himself a duke, and living a duke's life and parading in ducal fuss and feathers, when he was n't a duke at all, and could find it out if he would only examine the herald's records.

Y. M. But anyway, he is obliged to do a duke's part; he puts his hand in his pocket and does his benevolences on as big a scale as he can stand, and that benefits the community.

O. M. He could do that without being a duke.

Y. M. But would he?

O. M. Don't you see where you are arriving?

Y. M. Where?

O. M. At the standpoint of the other schemes: That it is good morals to let an ignorant duke do showy benevolences for his pride's sake, a pretty low motive, and go on doing them unwarned, lest if he were made acquainted with the actual motive which prompted them he might shut up his purse and cease to be good?

Y. M. But is n't it best to leave him in ignorance, as long as he *thinks* he is doing good for others' sake?

O. M. Perhaps so. It is the position of the other schemes. They think humbug is good enough morals when the dividend on it is good deeds and handsome conduct.

Y. M. It is my opinion that under your scheme of a man's doing a good deed for his *own* sake first-off, instead of first for the *good deed's* sake, no man would ever do one.

O. M. Have you committed a benevolence lately?

Y. M. Yes. This morning.

O. M. Give the particulars.

Y. M. The cabin of the old negro woman who used

to nurse me when I was a child and who saved my life once at the risk of her own, was burned last night, and she came mourning this morning, and pleading for money to build another one.

O. M. You furnished it?

Y. M. Certainly.

O. M. You were glad you had the money?

Y. M. Money? I had n't it. I sold my horse.

O. M. You were glad you had the horse?

Y. M. Of course I was; for if I had n't had the horse I should have been incapable, and my *mother* would have captured the chance to set old Sally up.

O. M. You were cordially glad you were not caught out and incapable?

Y. M. Oh, I just was!

O. M. Now, then—

Y. M. Stop where you are! I know your whole catalogue of questions, and I could answer every one of them without your wasting the time to ask them; but I will summarize the whole thing in a single remark: I did the charity knowing it was because the act would give *me* a splendid pleasure, and because old Sally's moving gratitude and delight would give *me* another one; and because the reflection that she would be happy now and out of her trouble would fill *me* full of happiness. I did the whole thing with my eyes open and recognizing and realizing that I was looking out for *my* share of the profits *first*. Now then, I have confessed. Go on.

O. M. I have n't anything to offer; you have covered the whole ground. Could you have been any *more* strongly moved to help Sally out of her trouble —could you have done the deed any more eagerly— if you had been under the delusion that you were doing it for *her* sake and profit only?

Y. M. No! Nothing in the world could have made the impulse which moved me more powerful, more masterful, more thoroughly irresistible. I played the limit!

O. M. Very well. You begin to suspect—and I claim to *know*—that when a man is a shade *more strongly moved* to do *one* of two things or of two dozen things than he is to do any one of the *others*, he will infallibly do that *one* thing, be it good or be it evil; and if it be good, not all the beguilements of all the casuistries can increase the strength of the impulse by a single shade or add a shade to the comfort and contentment he will get out of the act.

Y. M. Then you believe that such tendency toward doing good as is in men's hearts would not be diminished by the removal of the delusion that good deeds are done primarily for the sake of No. 2 instead of for the sake of No. 1?

O. M. That is what I fully believe.

Y. M. Does n't it somehow seem to take from the dignity of the deed?

O. M. If there is dignity in falsity, it does. It removes that.

Y. M. What is left for the moralist to do?

O. M. Teach unreservedly what he already teaches with one side of his mouth and takes back with the other: Do right *for your own sake,* and be happy in knowing that your *neighbor* will certainly share in the benefits resulting.

Y. M. Repeat your Admonition.

O. M. *Diligently train your ideals upward and still upward toward a summit where you will find your chiefest pleasure in conduct which, while contenting you, will be sure to confer benefits upon your neighbor and the community.*

Y. M. One's *every* act proceeds from *exterior influences,* you think?

O. M. Yes.

Y. M. If I conclude to rob a person, I am not the *originator* of the idea, but it comes in from the *outside?* I see him handling money—for instance—and *that* moves me to the crime?

O. M. That, by itself? Oh, certainly not. It is merely the *latest* outside influence of a procession of preparatory influences stretching back over a period of years. No *single* outside influence can make a man do a thing which is at war with his training. The most it can do is to start his mind on a new track and open it to the reception of *new* influences —as in the case of Ignatius Loyola. In time these influences can train him to a point where it will be consonant with his new character to yield to the *final* influence and do that thing. I will put the case in a form which will make my theory clear to you, I think. Here are two ingots of virgin gold. They shall represent a couple of characters which have been refined and perfected in the virtues by years of diligent right training. Suppose you wanted to break down these strong and well compacted characters— what influence would you bring to bear upon the ingots?

Y. M. Work it out yourself. Proceed.

O. M. Suppose I turn upon one of them a steam-jet during a long succession of hours. Will there be a result?

Y. M. None that I know of.

O. M. Why?

Y. M. A steam-jet cannot break down such a substance.

O. M. Very well. The steam is an *outside influence*, but it is ineffective, because the gold *takes no interest in it*. The ingot remains as it was. Suppose we add to the steam some quicksilver in a vaporized condition, and turn the jet upon the ingot, will there be an instantaneous result?

Y. M. No.

O. M. The *quicksilver* is an outside influence which gold (by its peculiar nature—say *temperament, disposition*), *cannot be indifferent to*. It stirs the interest of the gold, although we do not perceive it; but a *single* application of the influence works no damage. Let us continue the application in a steady stream, and call each minute a year. By the end of ten or twenty minutes—ten or twenty years—the little ingot is sodden with quicksilver, its virtues are gone, its character is degraded. At last it is ready to yield to a temptation which it would have taken no notice of, ten or twenty years ago. We will apply that temptation in the form of a pressure of my finger. You note the result?

Y.M. Yes; the ingot has crumbled to sand. I understand, now. It is not the *single* outside influence that does the work, but only the *last* one of a long and disintegrating accumulation of them. I see, now, how my *single* impulse to rob the man is not the one that makes me do it, but only the *last* one of a preparatory series. You might illustrate it with a parable.

A PARABLE

O. M. I will. There was once a pair of New England boys—twins. They were alike in good dispositions, fleckless morals, and personal appearance. They were the models of the Sunday-school. At fifteen George had an opportunity to go as cabin-boy in a whale-ship, and sailed away for the Pacific. Henry remained at home in the village. At eighteen George was a sailor before the mast, and Henry was teacher of the advanced Bible class. At twenty-two George, through fighting-habits and drinking-habits acquired at sea and in the sailor boarding-houses of the European and Oriental ports, was a common rough in Hong Kong, and out of a job; and Henry was superintendent of the Sunday-school. At twenty-six George was a wanderer, a tramp, and Henry was pastor of the village church. Then

George came home, and was Henry's guest. One evening a man passed by and turned down the lane, and Henry said, with a pathetic smile, "Without intending me a discomfort, that man is always keeping me reminded of my pinching poverty, for he carries heaps of money about him, and goes by here every evening of his life." That *outside influence*—that remark—was enough for George, but *it* was not the one that made him ambush the man and rob him, it merely represented the eleven years' accumulation of such influences, and gave birth to the act for which their long gestation had made preparation. It had never entered the head of Henry to rob the man—his ingot had been subjected to clean steam only; but George's had been subjected to vaporized quicksilver.

V

More About the Machine

Note.—When Mrs. W. asks how can a millionaire give a single dollar to colleges and museums while one human being is destitute of bread; she has answered her question herself. Her feeling for the poor shows that she has a standard of benevolence; therefore she has conceded the millionaire's privilege of having a standard; since she evidently requires him to adopt her standard she is by that act requiring herself to adopt his. The human being always looks down when he is examining another person's standard, he never finds one that he has to examine by looking up.

THE MAN-MACHINE AGAIN

Y. M. You really think man is a mere machine?

O. M. I do.

Y. M. And that his mind works automatically and is independent of his control—carries on thought on its own hook?

O. M. Yes. It is diligently at work, unceasingly at work, during every waking moment. Have you never tossed about all night, imploring, beseeching, commanding your mind to stop work and let you go to sleep?—you who perhaps imagine that your mind is your servant and must obey your orders, think what you tell it to think, and stop when you tell it to stop. When it chooses to work, there is no way to keep it still for an instant. The brightest man would not be able to supply it with subjects if he had to hunt them up. If it needed the man's help it would wait for him to give it work when he wakes in the morning.

Y. M. Maybe it does.

O. M. No, it begins right away, before the man gets wide enough awake to give it a suggestion. He may go to sleep saying, "The moment I wake I will think upon such and such a subject," but he will fail. His mind will be too quick for him; by the time he has become nearly enough awake to be half conscious, he will find that it is already at work upon another subject. Make the experiment and see.

Y. M. At any rate he can make it stick to a subject if he wants to.

O. M. Not if it finds another that suits it better. As a rule it will listen to neither a dull speaker nor a bright one. It refuses all persuasion. The dull speaker wearies it and sends it far away in idle dreams; the bright speaker throws out stimulating ideas which it goes chasing after and is at once unconscious of him and his talk. You cannot keep your mind from wandering, if it wants to; it is master, not you.

After an Interval of Days

O. M. Now, dreams—but we will examine that later. Meantime, did you try commanding your mind to wait for orders from you, and not do any thinking on its own hook?

Y. M. Yes, I commanded it to stand ready to take orders when I should wake in the morning.

O. M. Did it obey?

Y. M. No. It went to thinking of something of its own initiation, without waiting for me. Also—as you suggested—at night I appointed a theme for it to begin on in the morning, and commanded it to begin on that one and no other.

O. M. Did it obey?

Y. M. No.

O. M. How many times did you try the experiment?

Y. M. Ten.

O. M. How many successes did you score?

Y. M. Not one.

O. M. It is as I have said: the mind is independent of the man. He has no control over it, it does as it pleases. It will take up a subject in spite of him; it will stick to it in spite of him; it will throw it aside in spite of him. It is entirely independent of him.

Y. M. Go on. Illustrate.

O. M. Do you know chess?

Y. M. I learned it a week ago.

O. M. Did your mind go on playing the game all night that first night?

Y. M. Don't mention it!

O. M. It was eagerly, unsatisfiably interested; it rioted in the combinations; you implored it to drop the game and let you get some sleep?

Y. M. Yes. It would n't listen; it played right along. It wore me out and I got up haggard and wretched in the morning.

O. M. At some time or other you have been captivated by a ridiculous rhyme-jingle?

Y. M. Indeed, yes!

> "I saw Esau kissing Kate,
> And she saw I saw Esau;
> I saw Esau, he saw Kate,
> And she saw ——"

And so on. My mind went mad with joy over it. It repeated it all day and all night for a week in spite of all I could do to stop it, and it seemed to me that I must surely go crazy.

O. M. And the new popular song?

Y. M. Oh, yes! "In the Swee-eet By and By"; etc. Yes, the new popular song with the taking melody sings thro' one's head day and night, asleep and awake, till one is a wreck. There is no getting the mind to let it alone.

O. M. Yes, asleep as well as awake. The mind is quite independent. It is master. You have nothing to do with it. It is so apart from you that it can conduct its affairs, sing its songs, play its chess, weave its complex and ingeniously-constructed dreams, while you sleep. It has no use for your help, no use for your guidance, and never uses either, whether you be asleep or awake. You have imagined that you could originate a thought in your mind, and you have sincerely believed you could do it.

Y. M. Yes, I have had that idea.

O. M. Yet you can't originate a dream-thought for it to work out, and get it accepted?

Y. M. No.

O. M. And you can't dictate its procedure after it has originated a dream-thought for itself?

Y. M. No. No one can do it. Do you think the waking mind and the dream-mind are the same machine?

O. M. There is argument for it. We have wild

and fantastic day-thoughts? Things that are dream-like?

Y. M. Yes—like Mr. Wells's man who invented a drug that made him invisible; and like the Arabian tales of the Thousand Nights.

O. M. And there are dreams that are rational, simple, consistent and unfantastic?

Y. M. Yes. I have dreams that are like that. Dreams that are just like real life; dreams in which there are several persons with distinctly differentiated characters—inventions of my mind and yet strangers to me: a vulgar person; a refined one; a wise person; a fool; a cruel person; a kind and compassionate one; a quarrelsome person; a peacemaker; old persons and young; beautiful girls and homely ones. They talk in character, each preserves his own characteristics. There are vivid fights, vivid and biting insults, vivid love-passages; there are tragedies and comedies, there are griefs that go to one's heart, there are sayings and doings that make you laugh: indeed, the whole thing is exactly like real life.

O. M. Your dreaming mind originates the scheme, consistently and artistically develops it, and carries the little drama creditably through—all without help or suggestion from you?

Y. M. Yes.

O. M. It is argument that it could do the like awake without help or suggestion from you—and I think it does. It is argument that it is the same old mind in both cases, and never needs your help. I think the mind is purely a machine, a thoroughly independent machine, an automatic machine. Have you tried the other experiment which I suggested to you?

Y. M. Which one?

O. M. The one which was to determine how much influence you have over your mind—if any.

Y. M. Yes, and got more or less entertainment out of it. I did as you ordered: I placed two texts before my eyes—one a dull one and barren of interest, the other one full of interest, inflamed with it, white-hot with it. I commanded my mind to busy itself solely with the dull one.

O. M. Did it obey?

Y. M. Well, no, it did n't. It busied itself with the other one.

O. M. Did you try hard to make it obey?

Y. M. Yes, I did my honest best.

O. M. What was the text which it refused to be interested in or think about?

Y. M. It was this question: If A owes B a dollar and a half, and B owes C two and three-quarters,

and C owes A thirty-five cents, and D and A together owe E and B three-sixteenths of—of—I
don't remember the rest, now, but anyway it was
wholly uninteresting, and I could not force my mind
to stick to it even half a minute at a time; it kept flying off to the other text.

o. m. What was the other text?

y. m. It is no matter about that.

o. m. But what was it?

y. m. A photograph.

o. m. Your own?

y. m. No. It was hers.

o. m. You really made an honest good test. Did
you make a second trial?

y. m. Yes. I commanded my mind to interest
itself in the morning paper's report of the pork
market, and at the same time I reminded it of an experience of mine of 16 years ago. It refused to consider the pork, and gave its whole blazing interest
to that ancient incident.

o. m. What was the incident?

y. m. An armed desperado slapped my face in
the presence of twenty spectators. It makes me
wild and murderous every time I think of it.

o. m. Good tests, both; very good tests. Did
you try my other suggestion?

y. m. The one which was to prove to me that if I

would leave my mind to its own devices it would find things to think about without any of my help, and thus convince me that it was a machine, an automatic machine, set in motion by exterior influences, and as independent of me as it could be if it were in some one else's skull?   Is that the one?

O. M. Yes.

Y. M. I tried it.   I was shaving. I had slept well, and my mind was very lively, even gay and frisky. It was reveling in a fantastic and joyful episode of my remote boyhood which had suddenly flashed up in my memory,—moved to this by the spectacle of a yellow cat picking its way carefully along the top of the garden wall. The color of this cat brought the bygone cat before me, and I saw her walking along the sidestep of the pulpit; saw her walk onto a large sheet of sticky fly-paper and get all her feet involved; saw her struggle and fall down, helpless and dissatisfied, more and more urgent, more and more unreconciled, more and more mutely profane; saw the silent congregation quivering like jelly, and the tears running down their faces.   I saw it all.   The sight of the tears whisked my mind to a far distant and a sadder scene—in Terra del Fuego—and with Darwin's eyes I saw a naked great savage hurl his little boy against the rocks for a trifling fault; saw the poor mother gather up her dying child and hug it to her breast and weep, uttering no word. Did my mind stop to mourn with that nude black sister of mine? No—it was far away from that scene in an instant, and was busying itself with an ever-recurring and disagreeable dream of mine. In this dream I always find myself, stripped to my shirt, cringing and dodging about in the midst of a great drawing-room throng of finely dressed ladies and gentlemen, and wondering how I got there. And so on and so on, picture after picture, incident after incident, a drifting panorama of ever-changing, ever-dissolving views manufactured by my mind without any help from me—why, it would take me two hours to merely name the multitude of things my mind tallied off and photographed in fifteen minutes, let alone describe them to you.

O. M. A man's mind, left free, has no use for his help. But there is one way whereby he can get its help when he desires it.

Y. M. What is that way?

O. M. When your mind is racing along from subject to subject and strikes an inspiring one, open your mouth and begin talking upon that matter—or take your pen and use that. It will interest your mind and concentrate it, and it will pursue the sub-

ject with satisfaction.   It will take full charge, and
furnish the words itself.

Y. M. But don't I tell it what to say?

O. M. There are certainly occasions when you
have n't time.   The words leap out before you know
what is coming.

Y. M. For instance?

O. M. Well, take a "flash of wit"—repartee.
Flash is the right word.   It is out instantly.   There
is no time to arrange the words.   There is no thinking, no reflecting.   Where there is a wit-mechanism
it is automatic in its action, and needs no help.
Where the wit-mechanism is lacking, no amount of
study and reflection can manufacture the product.

Y. M. You really think a man originates nothing,
creates nothing.

THE THINKING-PROCESS

O. M. I do.   Men perceive, and their brain-
machines automatically combine the things per-
ceived.   That is all.

Y. M. The steam engine?

O. M. It takes fifty men a hundred years to invent it. One meaning of invent is discover. I use the word in that sense. Little by little they discover and apply the multitude of details that go to make the perfect engine. Watt noticed that confined steam was strong enough to lift the lid of the tea-pot. He did n't create the idea, he merely discovered the fact; the cat had noticed it a hundred times. From the tea-pot he evolved the cylinder—from the displaced lid he evolved the piston-rod. To attach something to the piston-rod to be moved by it, was a simple matter—crank and wheel. And so there was a working engine.[1]

One by one, improvements were discovered by men who used their eyes, not their creating powers— for they had n't any—and now, after a hundred years the patient contributions of fifty or a hundred observers stand compacted in the wonderful machine which drives the ocean liner.

Y. M. A Shakespearean play?

O. M. The process is the same. The first actor was a savage. He reproduced in his theatrical war-dances, scalp-dances, and so on, incidents which he had seen in real life. A more advanced civilization produced more incidents, more episodes; the actor

[1] The Marquess of Worcester had done all of this more than a century earlier.

and the story-teller borrowed them. And so the drama grew, little by little, stage by stage. It is made up of the facts of life, not creations. It took centuries to develop the Greek drama. It borrowed from preceding ages; it lent to the ages that came after. Men observe and combine, that is all. So does a rat.

Y. M. How?

O. M. He observes a smell, he infers a cheese, he seeks and finds. The astronomer observes this and that; adds his this and that to the this-and-thats of a hundred predecessors, infers an invisible planet, seeks it and finds it. The rat gets into a trap; gets out with trouble; infers that cheese in traps lacks value, and meddles with that trap no more. The astronomer is very proud of his achievement, the rat is proud of his. Yet both are machines, they have done machine work, they have originated nothing, they have no right to be vain, the whole credit belongs to their Maker. They are entitled to no honors, no praises, no monuments when they die, no remembrance. One is a complex and elaborate machine, the other a simple and limited machine, but they are alike in principle, function and process, and neither of them works otherwise than automatically, and neither of them may righteously claim a *personal* superiority or a personal dignity above the other.

Y. M. In earned personal dignity, then, and in personal merit for what he does, it follows of necessity that he is on the same level as a rat?

O. M. His brother the rat; yes, that is how it seems to me. Neither of them being entitled to any personal merit for what he does, it follows of necessity that neither of them has a right to arrogate to himself (personally-created) superiorities over his brother.

Y. M. Are you determined to go on believing in these insanities? Would you go on believing in them in the face of able arguments backed by collated facts and instances?

O. M. I have been a humble, earnest and sincere Truth-Seeker.

Y. M. Very well?

O. M. The humble, earnest and sincere Truth-Seeker is always convertible by such means.

Y. M. I am thankful to God to hear you say this, for now I know that your conversion—

O. M. Wait. You misunderstand. I said I have *been* a Truth-Seeker.

Y. M. Well?

O. M. I am not that now. Have you forgotten? I told you that there are none but temporary Truth-Seekers; that a permanent one is a human impossibility; that as soon as the Seeker finds what he is thoroughly convinced is the Truth, he seeks no further, but gives the rest of his days to hunting junk to patch it and caulk it and prop it with, and make it weather-proof and keep it from caving in on him. Hence the Presbyterian remains a Presbyterian, the Mohammedan a Mohammedan, the Spiritualist a Spiritualist, the Democrat a Democrat, the Republican a Republican, the Monarchist a Monarchist; and if a humble, earnest and sincere Seeker after Truth should find it in the proposition that the moon is made of green cheese nothing could ever budge him from that position; for he is nothing but an automatic machine, and must obey the laws of his construction.

Y. M. And so—

O. M. Having found the Truth; perceiving that beyond question man has but one moving impulse—the contenting of his own spirit—and is merely a machine and entitled to no personal merit for anything he does, it is not humanly possible for me to seek further. The rest of my days will be spent in patching and painting and puttying and caulking my priceless possession and in looking the other way when an imploring argument or a damaging fact approaches.

INSTINCT AND THOUGHT

VI

Instinct and Thought

Y. M. It is odious. Those drunken theories of yours, advanced a while ago—concerning the rat and all that—strip Man bare of all his dignities, grandeurs, sublimities.

O. M. He has n't any to strip—they are shams, stolen clothes. He claims credits which belong solely to his Maker.

Y. M. But you have no right to put him on a level with a rat.

O. M. I don't—morally. That would not be fair to the rat. The rat is well above him, there.

Y. M. Are you joking?

O. M. No, I am not.

Y. M. Then what do you mean?

O. M. That comes under the head of the Moral Sense. It is a large question. Let us finish with what we are about now, before we take it up.

Y. M. Very well. You have seemed to concede that you place Man and the rat on *a* level. What is it? The intellectual?

O. M. In form—not in degree.

Y. M. Explain.

O. M. I think that the rat's mind and the man's mind are the same machine, but of unequal capacities—like yours and 'Edison's; like the African pigmy's and Homer's; like the Bushman's and Bismarck's.

Y. M. How are you going to make that out, when the lower animals have no mental quality but instinct, while man possesses reason?

O. M. What is instinct?

Y. M. It is merely unthinking and mechanical exercise of inherited habit.

O. M. What originated the habit?

Y. M. The first animal started it, its descendants have inherited it.

O. M. How did the first one come to start it?

Y. M. I don't know; but it did n't *think* it out.

O. M. How do you know it did n't?

Y. M. Well—I have a right to suppose it did n't, anyway.

O. M. I don't believe you have. What is thought?

Y. M. I know what you call it: the mechanical and automatic putting together of impressions received from outside, and drawing an inference from them.

O. M. Very good. Now my idea of the meaningless term "instinct" is, that it is merely *petrified thought;* solidified and made inanimate by habit; thought which was once alive and awake, but is become unconscious—walks in its sleep, so to speak.

Y. M. Illustrate it.

O. M. Take a herd of cows, feeding in a pasture. Their heads are all turned in one direction. They do that instinctively; they gain nothing by it, they have no reason for it, they don't know why they do it. It is an inherited habit which was originally thought—that is to say, observation of an exterior fact, and a valuable inference drawn from that observation and confirmed by experience. The original wild ox noticed that with the wind in his favor he could smell his enemy in time to escape; then he inferred that it was worth while to keep his nose to the wind. That is the process which man calls reasoning. Man's thought-machine works just like the other animals', but it is a better one and more Edisonian. Man, in the ox's place, would go further, reason wider: he would face part of the herd the other way and protect both front and rear.

Y. M. Did you say the term instinct is meaningless?

O. M. I think it is a bastard word. I think it confuses us; for as a rule it applies itself to habits and impulses which had a far-off origin in thought, and now and then breaks the rule and applies itself to habits which can hardly claim a thought-origin.

Y. M. Give an instance.

O. M. Well, in putting on trousers a man always inserts the same old leg first—never the other one. There is no advantage in that, and no sense in it. All men do it, yet no man thought it out and adopted it of set purpose, I imagine. But it is a habit which is transmitted, no doubt, and will continue to be transmitted.

Y. M. Can you prove that the habit exists?

O. M. You can prove it, if you doubt. If you will take a man to a clothing store and watch him try on a dozen pairs of trousers, you will see.

Y. M. The cow-illustration is not—

O. M. Sufficient to show that a dumb animal's mental machine is just the same as a man's and its reasoning processes the same? I will illustrate further. If you should hand Mr. Edison a box which you caused to fly open by some concealed device, he would infer a spring, and would hunt for it and find it. Now an uncle of mine had an old horse who used to get into the closed lot where the corn-crib was and dishonestly take the corn. I got the punishment myself, as it was supposed that I had heedlessly failed to insert the wooden pin which kept the gate closed. These persistent punishments fatigued me; they also caused me to infer the existence of a culprit, somewhere; so I hid myself and watched the gate. Presently the horse came and pulled the pin out with his teeth and went in. Nobody taught him that; he had observed—then thought it out for himself. His process did not differ from Edison's; he put this and that together and drew an inference—and the peg, too; but I made him sweat for it.

Y. M. It has something of the seeming of thought about it. Still it is not very elaborate. Enlarge.

O. M. Suppose that Edison has been enjoying some one's hospitalities. He comes again by and by, and the house is vacant. He infers that his host has moved. A while afterward, in another town, he sees the man enter a house; he infers that that is the new home, and follows to inquire. Here, now, is the experience of a gull, as related by a naturalist. The scene is a Scotch fishing village where the gulls were kindly treated. This particular gull visited a cottage; was fed; came next day and was fed again; came into the house, next time, and ate with the family; kept on doing this almost daily, thereafter. But, once the gull was away on a journey for a few days, and when it returned the house was vacant. Its friends had removed to a village three miles distant. Several months later it saw the head of the family on the street there, followed him home, entered the house without excuse or apology, and became a daily guest again. Gulls do not rank high, mentally, but this one had memory and the reasoning faculty, you see, and applied them Edisonially.

Y. M. Yet it was not an Edison and could n't be developed into one.

O. M. Perhaps not; could you?

Y. M. That is neither here nor there. Go on.

O. M. If Edison were in trouble and a stranger helped him out of it and next day he got into the same difficulty again, he would infer the wise thing to do in case he knew the stranger's address. Here is a case of a bird and a stranger as related by a naturalist. An Englishman saw a bird flying around about his dog's head, down in the grounds, and uttering cries of distress. He went there to see about it. The dog had a young bird in his mouth—unhurt. The gentleman rescued it and put it on a bush and brought the dog away. Early the next morning the mother-bird came for the gentleman, who was sitting on his verandah, and by its manœuvers persuaded him to follow it to a distant part of the grounds—flying a little way in front of him and waiting for him to catch up, and so on; and keeping to the winding path, too, instead of flying the near way across lots. The distance covered was four hundred yards. The same dog was the culprit; he had the young bird again, and once more he had to give it up. Now the mother-bird had reasoned it all out: Since the stranger had helped her once, she inferred that he would do it again; she knew where to find him, and she went upon her errand with confidence. Her mental processes were what Edison's would have been. She put this and that together—and that is all that thought *is*—and out of them built her logical arrangement of inferences. Edison could n't have done it any better himself.

Y. M. Do you believe that many of the dumb animals can think?

O. M. Yes—the elephant, the monkey, the horse, the dog, the parrot, the macaw, the mocking-bird, and many others. The elephant whose mate fell into a pit, and who dumped dirt and rubbish into the pit till the bottom was raised high enough to enable the captive to step out, was equipped with the reasoning quality. I conceive that all animals that can learn things through teaching and drilling have to know how to observe, and put this and that together and draw an inference—the process of thinking. Could you teach an idiot the manual of arms, and to advance, retreat, and go through complex field manœuvers at the word of command?

Y. M. Not if he were a thorough idiot.

O. M. Well, canary birds can learn all that; dogs and elephants learn all sorts of wonderful things. They must surely be able to notice, and to put things together, and say to themselves, "I get the idea, now: when I do so and so, as per order, I am praised and fed; when I do differently I am punished." Fleas can be taught nearly anything that a Congressman can.

Y. M. Granting, then, that dumb animals are able to think upon a low plane, is there any that can think upon a high one? Is there one that is well up towards man?

O. M. Yes. As a thinker and planner the ant is the equal of any savage race of men; as a self-educated specialist in several arts she is the superior of any savage race of men; and in one or two high mental qualities she is above the reach of any man, savage or civilized.

Y. M. Oh, come! you are abolishing the intellectual frontier which separates man and beast.

O. M. I beg your pardon. One cannot abolish what does not exist.

Y. M. You are not in earnest I hope. You cannot mean to seriously say there is no such frontier.

O. M. I do say it seriously. The instances of the horse, the gull, the mother-bird and the elephant show that those creatures put their this's and thats together just as Edison would have done it and drew the same inferences that he would have drawn. Their mental machinery was just like his, also its manner of working. Their equipment was as inferior to his, in elaboration, as a Waterbury is inferior to the Strasburg clock, but that is the only difference—there is no frontier.

Y. M. It looks exasperatingly true; and is distinctly offensive. It elevates the dumb beasts to—to—

O. M. Let us drop that lying phrase, and call them the Unrevealed Creatures; so far as we can know, there is no such thing as a dumb beast.

Y. M. On what grounds do you make that assertion?

O. M. On quite simple ones. "Dumb" beast suggests an animal that has no thought-machinery, no understanding, no speech, no way of communicating what is in its mind. We know that a hen *has* speech. We cannot understand every thing she says, but we easily learn two or three of her phrases. We know when she is saying "I have laid an egg"; we know when she is saying to the chicks, "Run here, dears, I 've found a worm"; we know what she is saying when she voices a warning: "Quick! hurry! gather yourselves under mamma, there 's a hawk coming!" We understand the cat when she stretches herself out, purring with affection and contentment and lifts up a soft voice and says "Come, kitties, supper's ready"; we understand her when she goes mourning about and says "Where can they be?—they are lost—won't you help me hunt for them?" and we understand the disreputable Tom when he challenges at midnight from his shed: "You come over here, you product of immoral commerce, and I 'll make your fur fly!" We understand a few of a dog's phrases, and we learn to understand a few of the remarks and gestures of any bird or other animal that we domesticate and observe. The clearness and exactness of the few of the hen's speeches which we understand is argument that she can communicate to her kind a hundred things which

we cannot comprehend—in a word, that she can con-
verse. And this argument is also applicable in the
case of others of the great army of the Unrevealed.
It is just like man's vanity and impertinence to call
an animal dumb because it is dumb to his dull perceptions. Now as to the ant—

Y. M. Yes, go back to the ant, the creature that—
as you seem to think—sweeps away the last vestige
of an intellectual frontier between man and the Unrevealed.

O. M. That is what she surely does. In all his
history the aboriginal Australian never thought out
a house for himself and built it. The ant is an
amazing architect. She is a wee little creature, but
she builds a strong and enduring house eight feet
high—a house which is as large in proportion to her
size as is the largest capitol or cathedral in the
world compared to man's size. No savage race has
produced architects who could approach the ant in
genius or culture. No civilized race has produced
architects who could plan a house better for the
uses proposed than can hers. Her house contains
a throne-room; nurseries for her young; granaries;
apartments for her soldiers, her workers, etc.; and
they and the multifarious halls and corridors which
communicate with them are arranged and distributed

with an educated and experienced eye for convenience and adaptability.

Y. M. That could be mere instinct.

O. M. It would elevate the savage if he had it.
But let us look further before we decide. The ant
has soldiers—battalions, regiments, armies; and they
have their appointed captains and generals, who lead
them to battle.

Y. M. That could be instinct, too.

O. M. We will look still further. The ant has a
system of government; it is well planned, elaborate,
and is well carried on.

Y. M. Instinct again.

O. M. She has crowds of slaves, and is a hard and
unjust employer of forced labor.

Y. M. Instinct.

O. M. She has cows, and milks them.

Y. M. Instinct, of course.

O. M. In Texas she lays out a farm twelve feet
square, plants it, weeds it, cultivates it, gathers the
crop and stores it away.

Y. M. Instinct, all the same.

O. M. The ant discriminates between friend and
stranger. Sir John Lubbock took ants from two
different nests, made them drunk with whisky and
laid them, unconscious, by one of the nests, near

some water. Ants from the nest came and examined and discussed these disgraced creatures, then carried their friends home and threw the strangers overboard. Sir John repeated the experiment a number of times. For a time the sober ants did as they had done at first—carried their friends home and threw the strangers overboard. But finally they lost patience, seeing that their reformatory efforts went for nothing, and threw both friends and strangers overboard. Come—is this instinct, or is it thoughtful and intelligent discussion of a thing new—absolutely new—to their experience; with a verdict arrived at, sentence passed, and judgment executed? Is it instinct?—thought petrified by ages of habit—or is n't it brand-new thought, inspired by the new occasion, the new circumstances?

Y. M. I have to concede it. It was not a result of habit; it has all the look of reflection, thought, putting this and that together, as you phrase it. I believe it was thought.

O. M. I will give you another instance of thought. Franklin had a cup of sugar on a table in his room. The ants got at it. He tried several preventives; the ants rose superior to them. Finally he contrived one which shut off access—probably set the table's legs in pans of water, or drew a circle of tar around the cup, I don't remember. At any rate he watched to see what they would do. They tried various schemes—failures, every one. The ants were badly puzzled. Finally they held a consultation, discussed the problem, arrived at a decision—and this time they beat that great philosopher. They formed in procession, crossed the floor, climbed the wall, marched across the ceiling to a point just over the cup, then one by one they let go and fell down into it! Was that instinct—thought petrified by ages of inherited habit?

Y. M. No, I don't believe it was. I believe it was a newly-reasoned scheme to meet a new emergency.

O. M. Very well. You have conceded the reasoning power in two instances. I come now to a mental detail wherein the ant is a long way the superior of any human being. Sir John Lubbock proved by many experiments that an ant knows a stranger-ant of her own species in a moment, even when the stranger is disguised—with paint. Also he proved that an ant knows every individual in her hive of 500,000 souls. Also, after a year's absence of one of the 500,000 she will straightway recognize the returned absentee and grace the recognition with an affectionate welcome. How are these recognitions made? Not by color, for painted ants were recognized. Not by smell, for ants that had been dipped in chloroform were recognized. Not by speech and not by antennæ-signs nor contacts, for the drunken and motionless ants were recognized and the friend discriminated from the stranger. The ants were all of the same species, therefore the friends had to be recognized by form and feature—friends who formed part of a hive of 500,000! Has any man a memory for form and feature approaching that?

Y. M. Certainly not.

O. M. Franklin's ants and Lubbock's ants show fine capacities of putting this and that together in new and untried emergencies and deducting smart conclusions from the combinations—a man's mental process exactly. With memory to help, man preserves his observations and reasonings, reflects upon them, adds to them, re-combines, and so proceeds, stage by stage, to far results—from the tea-kettle to the ocean greyhound's complex engine; from personal labor to slave labor; from wigwam to palace; from the capricious chase to agriculture and stored food; from nomadic life to stable government and concentrated authority; from incoherent hordes to massed armies. The ant has observation, the reasoning faculty, and the preserving adjunct of a prodigious memory; she has duplicated man's development and the essential features of his civilization, and you call it all instinct!

Y. M. Perhaps I lacked the reasoning faculty myself.

O. M. Well, don't tell anybody, and don't do it again.

Y. M. We have come a good way.   As a result—as I understand it—I am required to concede that there is absolutely no intellectual frontier separating Man and the Unrevealed Creatures?

O. M. That is what you are required to concede. There is no such frontier—there is no way to get around that.   Man has a finer and more capable machine in him than those others, but it is the same machine and works in the same way.   And neither he nor those others can command the machine—it is strictly automatic, independent of control, works when it pleases, and when it does n't please, it can't be forced.

Y. M. Then man and the other animals are all alike, as to mental machinery, and there is n't any difference of any stupendous magnitude between them, except in quality, not in kind.

O. M. That is about the state of it—intellectuality. There are pronounced limitations on both sides.   We can't learn to understand much of their language, but the dog, the elephant, etc., learn to understand a very great deal of ours. To that extent they are our superiors. On the other hand they can't learn reading, writing, etc., nor any of our fine and high things, and there we have a large advantage over them.

Y. M. Very well, let them have what they 've got, and welcome; there is still a wall, and a lofty one. They have n't got the Moral Sense; we have it, and it lifts us immeasurably above them.

O. M. What makes you think that?

Y. M. Now look here—let us call a halt. I have stood the other infamies and insanities and that is enough; I am not going to have man and the other animals put on the same level morally.

O. M. I was n't going to hoist man up to that.

Y. M. This is too much! I think it is not right to jest about such things.

O. M. I am not jesting, I am merely reflecting a plain and simple truth—and without uncharitableness. The fact that man knows right from wrong proves his *intellectual* superiority to the other creatures; but the fact that he can *do* wrong proves his *moral* inferiority to any creature that *cannot*. It is my belief that this position is not assailable.

FREE WILL

Y. M. What is your opinion regarding Free Will?

O. M. That there is no such thing. Did the man possess it who gave the old woman his last shilling and trudged home in the storm?

Y. M. He had the choice between succoring the old woman and leaving her to suffer. Is n't it so?

O. M. Yes, there was a choice to be made, between bodily comfort on the one hand and the comfort of the spirit on the other. The body made a strong appeal, of course,—the body would be quite sure to do that; the spirit made a counter appeal. A choice had to be made between the two appeals, and was made. Who or what determined that choice?

Y. M. Any one but you would say that the man determined it, and that in doing it he exercised Free Will.

O. M. We are constantly assured that every man is endowed with Free Will, and that he can and must exercise it where he is offered a choice between good conduct and less-good conduct. Yet we clearly saw that in that man's case he really had no Free Will: his temperament, his training, and the daily influences which had moulded him and made him what he was, *compelled* him to rescue the old woman and thus save *himself*—save himself from spiritual pain, from unendurable wretchedness. He did not make the choice, it was made *for* him by forces which he could not control. Free Will has always existed in *words*, but it stops there, I think—stops short of *fact*. I would not use those words—Free Will—but others.

Y. M. What others?

O. M. Free Choice.

Y. M. What is the difference?

O. M. The one implies untrammeled power to *act* as you please, the other implies nothing beyond a mere *mental process:* the critical ability to determine which of two things is nearest right and just.

Y. M. Make the difference clear, please.

O. M. The mind can freely *select, choose, point out,* the right and just one—its function stops there. It can go no further in the matter. It has no authority to say that the right one shall be acted upon and the wrong one discarded. That authority is in other hands.

Y. M. The man's?

O. M. In the machine which stands for him. In his born disposition and the character which has been built around it by training and environment.

Y. M. It will act upon the right one of the two?

O. M. It will do as it pleases in the matter. George Washington's machine would act upon the right one; Pizarro's mind would know which was the right one and which the wrong, but the Master inside of Pizarro would act upon the wrong one.

Y. M. Then as I understand it a bad man's mental machinery calmly and judicially points out which of two things is right and just—

O. M. Yes, and his *moral* machinery will freely act upon the one or the other, according to its make, and be quite indifferent to the *mind's* feelings concerning the matter—that is, *would* be, if the mind had any feelings; which it has n't. It is merely a thermometer: it registers the heat and the cold, and cares not a farthing about either.

Y. M. Then we must not claim that if a man *knows* which of two things is right he is absolutely *bound* to do that thing?

O. M. His temperament and training will decide what he shall do, and he will do it; he cannot help himself, he has no authority over the matter. Was n't it right for David to go out and slay Goliath?

Y. M. Yes.

O. M. Then it would have been equally *right* for any one else to do it?

Y. M. Certainly.

O. M. Then it would have been *right* for a born coward to attempt it?

Y. M. It would—yes.

O. M. You know that no born coward ever would have attempted it, don't you?

Y. M. Yes.

O. M. You know that a born coward's make and temperament would be an absolute and insurmountable bar to his ever essaying such a thing, don't you?

Y. M. Yes, I know it.

O. M. He clearly perceives that it would be *right* to try it?

Y. M. Yes.

O. M. His mind has Free Choice in determining that it would be *right* to try it?

Y. M. Yes.

O. M. Then if by reason of his inborn cowardice he simply can *not* essay it, what becomes of his Free Will? Where is his Free Will? Why claim that he has Free Will when the plain facts show that he has n't? Why contend that because he and David *see* the right alike, both must *act* alike? Why impose the same laws upon goat and lion?

Y. M. There is really no such thing as Free Will?

O. M. It is what I think. There is *Will*. But it has nothing to do with *intellectual perceptions of right and wrong,* and is not under their command. David's temperament and training had Will, and it was a compulsory force; David had to obey its decrees, he had no choice. The coward's temperament and training possess Will, and *it* is compulsory; it commands him to avoid danger, and he obeys, he has no choice. But neither the Davids nor the cowards possess Free Will—will that may do the right or do the wrong, as their *mental* verdict shall decide.

NOT TWO VALUES, BUT ONLY ONE

Y. M. There is one thing which bothers me: I can't tell where you draw the line between *material* covetousness and *spiritual* covetousness.

O. M. I don't draw any.

Y. M. How do you mean?

O. M. There is no such thing as *material* covetousness. All covetousness is spiritual.

Y. M. *All* longings, desires, ambitions *spiritual,* never material?

O. M. Yes. The Master in you requires that in *all* cases you shall content his *spirit*—that alone. He never requires anything else, he never interests himself in any other matter.

Y. M. Ah, come! When he covets somebody's money—is n't that rather distinctly material and gross?

O. M. No. The money is merely a symbol—it represents in visible and concrete form a *spiritual desire.* Any so-called material thing that you want is merely a symbol: you want it not for *itself*, but because it will content your spirit for the moment.

Y. M. Please particularize.

O. M. Very well. Maybe the thing longed for is a new hat. You get it and your vanity is pleased, your spirit contented. Suppose your friends deride the hat, make fun of it: at once it loses its value; you are ashamed of it, you put it out of your sight, you never want to see it again.

Y. M. I think I see. Go on.

O. M. It is the same hat, is n't it? It is in no way altered. But it was n't the *hat* you wanted, but only what it stood for—a something to please and content your *spirit*. When it failed of that, the whole of its value was gone. There are no *material* values, there are only spiritual ones. You will hunt in vain for a material value that is *actual, real*—there is no such thing. The only value it possesses, for even a moment, is the spiritual value back of it: remove that and it is at once worthless—like the hat.

Y. M. Can you extend that to money?

O. M. Yes. It is merely a symbol, it has no *material* value; you think you desire it for its own sake, but it is not so. You desire it for the spiritual content it will bring; if it fail of that, you discover that its value is gone. There is that pathetic tale of the man who labored like a slave, unresting, unsatisfied, until he had accumulated a fortune, and was happy over it, jubilant about it; then in a single week a pestilence swept away all whom he held dear and left him desolate. His money's value was gone. He realized that his joy in it came not from the money itself, but from the spiritual contentment he got out of his family's enjoyment of the pleasures and delights it lavished upon them. Money has no *material* value; if you remove its spiritual value nothing is left but dross. It is so with all things, little or big, majestic or trivial—there are no exceptions. Crowns, sceptres, pennies, paste jewels, village notoriety, world-wide fame—they are all the same, they have no *material* value: while they content the *spirit* they are precious, when this fails they are worthless.

A DIFFICULT QUESTION

Y. M. You keep me confused and perplexed all the time by your elusive terminology. Sometimes you divide a man up into two or three separate personalities, each with authorities, jurisdictions and responsibilities of its own, and when he is in that condition I can't grasp him. Now when *I* speak of a man, he is *the whole thing in one*, and easy to hold and contemplate.

O. M. That is pleasant and convenient, if true. When you speak of "my body," who is the "my?"

Y. M. It is the "me."

O. M. The body is a property, then, and the Me owns it. Who is the Me?

Y. M. The Me is *the whole thing;* it is a common property; an undivided ownership, vested in the whole entity.

O. M. If the Me admires a rainbow, is it the whole Me that admires it, including the hair, hands, heels and all?

Y. M. Certainly not. It is my *mind* that admires it.

O. M. So *you* divide the Me yourself. Everybody does; everybody must. What, then, definitely, is the Me?

Y. M. I think it must consist of just those two parts—the body and the mind.

O. M. You think so? If you say "I believe the world is round," who is the "I" that is speaking?

Y. M. The mind.

O. M. If you say "I grieve for the loss of my father," who is the "I"?

Y. M. The mind.

O. M. Is the mind exercising an intellectual function when it examines and accepts the evidence that the world is round?

Y. M. Yes.

O. M. Is it exercising an intellectual function when it grieves for the loss of your father?

Y. M. No. That is not cerebration, brain-work, it is a matter of *feeling*.

O. M. Then its source is not in your mind, but in your *moral* territory?

Y. M. I have to grant it.

O. M. Is your mind a part of your *physical* equipment?

Y. M. No. It is independent of it; it is spiritual.

O. M. Being spiritual, it cannot be affected by physical influences?

Y. M. No.

O. M. Does the mind remain sober when the body is drunk?

Y. M. Well—no.

O. M. There *is* a physical effect present then?

Y. M. It looks like it.

O. M. A cracked skull has resulted in a crazy mind. Why should that happen if the mind is spiritual, and *independent* of physical influences?

Y. M. Well—I don't know.

O. M. When you have a pain in your foot, how do you know it?

Y. M. I feel it.

O. M. But you do not feel it until a nerve reports the hurt to the brain. Yet the brain is the seat of the mind, is it not?

Y. M. I think so.

O. M. But is n't spiritual enough to learn what is happening in the outskirts without the help of the *physical* messenger? You perceive that the question of who or what the Me is, is not a simple one at all. You say "I admire the rainbow," and "I believe the world is round," and in these cases we find that the Me is not all speaking, but only the *mental* part. You say "I grieve," and again the Me is not all speaking, but only the *moral* part. You say the mind is wholly spiritual; then you say "I have a pain" and find that this time the Me is mental *and* spiritual combined. We all use the "I" in this indeterminate fashion, there is no help for it. We imagine a Master and King over what you call The Whole Thing, and we speak of him as "I," but when we try to define him we find we cannot do it. The intellect and the feelings can act quite *independently* of each other; we recognize that, and we look around for a Ruler who is master over both, and can serve as a *definite and indisputable "I,"* and enable us to know what we mean and who or what we are talking about when we use that pronoun, but we have to give it up and confess that we cannot find him. To me, Man is a machine, made up of many mechanisms; the moral and mental ones acting automatically in accordance with the impulses of an interior Master who is built out of born-temperament and an accumulation of multitudinous outside influences and trainings; a machine whose *one* function is to secure the spiritual contentment of the Master, be his desires good or be they evil; a machine whose Will is absolute and must be obeyed, and always *is* obeyed.

Y. M. Maybe the Me is the Soul?

O. M. Maybe it is. What is the Soul?

Y. M. I don't know.

O. M. Neither does any one else.

THE MASTER-PASSION

Y. M. What is the Master?—or, in common speech the Conscience? Explain it.

O. M. It is that mysterious autocrat, lodged in a man, which compels the man to content its desires. It may be called the Master Passion—the hunger for Self-Approval.

Y. M. Where is its seat?

O. M. In man's moral constitution.

Y. M. Are its commands for the man's good?

O. M. It is indifferent to the man's good; it never concerns itself about anything but the satisfying of its own desires. It can be *trained* to prefer things which will be for the man's good, but it will prefer them only because they will content *it* better than other things would.

Y. M. Then even when it is trained to high ideals it is still looking out for its own contentment, and not for the man's good?

O. M. True. Trained or untrained, it cares noth-

ing for the man's good, and never concerns itself
about it.

Y. M. It seems to be an *immoral* force seated in
the man's moral constitution?

O. M. It is a *colorless* force seated in the man's
moral constitution.   Let us call it an instinct— a
blind, unreasoning instinct, which cannot and does
not distinguish between good morals and bad ones,
and cares nothing for results to the man provided
its own contentment be secured; and it will *always*
secure that.

Y. M. It seeks money, and it probably considers
that that is an advantage for the man?

O. M. It is not always seeking money, it is not always seeking power, nor office,   nor   any   other
material advantage.   In *all* cases it seeks a *spiritual*
contentment, let the *means* be what they may.   Its
desires are determined by the man's temperament—
and it is lord over that.   Temperament, Conscience,
Susceptibility, Spiritual Appetite, are in fact the
same thing.   Have you ever heard of a person who
cared nothing for money?

Y. M. Yes.   A scholar who would not leave his
garret and his books to take a place in a business
house at a large salary.

O. M. He had to satisfy his master,—that is to

say, his temperament, his Spiritual Appetite—and it preferred the books to money. Are there other cases?

Y. M. Yes, the hermit.

O. M. It is a good instance. The hermit endures solitude, hunger, cold, and manifold perils, to content his autocrat, who prefers these things, and prayer and contemplation, to money or to any show or luxury that money can buy. Are there others?

Y. M. Yes. The artist, the poet, the scientist.

O. M. Their autocrat prefers the deep pleasures of these occupations, either well paid or ill paid, to any others in the market, at any price. You *realize* that the Master Passion—the contentment of the spirit—concerns itself with many things besides so-called material advantage, material prosperity, cash, and all that?

Y. M. I think I must concede it.

O. M. I believe you must. There are perhaps as many Temperaments that would refuse the burdens and vexations and distinctions of public office as there are that hunger after them. The one set of Temperaments seek the contentment of the spirit, and that alone; and this is exactly the case with the other set. Neither set seeks anything *but* the contentment of the spirit. If the one is sordid, both are sordid; and equally so, since the end in view is precisely the same in both cases. And in both cases Temperament decides the preference—and Temperament is *born*, not made.

CONCLUSION

O. M. You have been taking a holiday?

Y. M. Yes; a mountain-tramp covering a week. Are you ready to talk?

O. M. Quite ready. What shall we begin with?

Y. M. Well, lying abed resting-up, two days and nights, I have thought over all these talks, and passed them carefully in review. With this result: That . . that . . are you intending to publish your notions about Man some day?

O. M. Now and then, in these past twenty years, the Master inside of me has half-intended to order me to set them to paper and publish them. Do I have to tell you why the order has remained unissued, or can you explain so simple a thing without my help?

Y. M. By your doctrine, it is simplicity itself: Outside influences moved your interior Master to give the order; stronger outside influences deterred him. Without the outside influences, neither of these impulses could ever have been born, since a person's brain is incapable of originating an idea within itself.

O. M. Correct. Go on.

Y. M. The matter of publishing or withholding is still in your Master's hands. If some day, an outside influence shall determine him to publish, he will give the order, and it will be obeyed.

O. M. That is correct. Well?

Y. M. Upon reflection I have arrived at the conviction that the publication of your doctrines would be harmful. Do you pardon me?

O. M. Pardon *you?* You have done nothing. You are an instrument—a speaking-trumpet. Speaking-trumpets are not responsible for what is said through them. Outside influences—in the form of life-long teachings, trainings, notions, prejudices, and other second-hand importations—have persuaded the Master within you that the publication of these doctrines would be harmful. Very well, this is quite natural, and was to be expected; in fact was inevitable. Go on; for the sake of ease and convenience, stick to habit: speak in the first person, and tell me what your Master thinks about it.

Y. M. Well to begin: it is a desolating doctrine; it is not inspiring, enthusing, uplifting. It takes the glory out of man, it takes the pride out of him, it takes the heroism out of him, it denies him all personal credit, all applause; it not only degrades him to a machine, but allows him no control over the machine; makes a mere coffee-mill of him, and neither permits him to supply the coffee nor turn the crank; his sole and piteously humble function being to grind coarse or fine, according to his make, outside impulses doing all the rest.

O. M. It is correctly stated. Tell me—what do men admire most in each other?

Y. M. Intellect, courage, majesty of build, beauty of countenance, charity, benevolence, magnanimity, kindliness, heroism, and—and—

O. M. I would not go any further. These are *elementals*. Virtue, fortitude, holiness, truthfulness, loyalty, high ideals—these, and all the related qualities that are named in the dictionary, are *made out of the elementals*, by blendings, combinations, and shadings of the elementals, just as one makes green by blending blue and yellow, and makes several shades and tints of red by modifying the elemental red. There are seven elemental colors, they are all in the rainbow; out of them we manufacture and name fifty shades of them. You have named the elementals of the human rainbow, and also one *blend*—heroism, which is made out of courage and magnanimity. Very well, then; which of these elements does the possessor of it manufacture for himself? Is it intellect?

Y. M. No.

O. M. Why?

Y. M. He is born with it.

O. M. Is it courage?

Y. M. No. He is born with it.

O. M. Is it majesty of build, beauty of countenance?

Y. M. No. They are birthrights.

O. M. Take those others—the elemental moral qualities—charity, benevolence, magnanimity, kindliness; fruitful seeds, out of which spring, through cultivation by outside influences, all the manifold blends and combinations of virtues named in the dictionaries: does man manufacture any one of those seeds, or are they all born in him?

Y. M. Born in him.

O. M. Who manufactures them, then?

Y. M. God.

O. M. Where does the credit of it belong?

Y. M. To God.

o. m. And the glory of which you spoke, and the applause?

y. m. To God.

o. m. Then it is *you* who degrade man. You make him claim glory, praise, flattery, for every valuable thing he possesses—*borrowed* finery, the whole of it; no rag of it earned by himself, not a detail of it produced by his own labor. *You* make man a humbug; have I done worse by him?

y. m. You have made a machine of him.

o. m. Who devised that cunning and beautiful mechanism, a man's hand?

y. m. God.

o. m. Who devised the law by which it automatically hammers out of a piano an elaborate piece of music, without error, while the man is thinking about something else, or talking to a friend?

y. m. God.

o. m. Who devised the blood? Who devised the wonderful machinery which automatically drives its renewing and refreshing streams through the body, day and night, without assistance or advice from the man? Who devised the man's mind, whose machinery works automatically, interests itself in what it pleases, regardless of his will or desire, labors all night when it likes, deaf to his appeals for mercy? God devised all these thing. *I* have not made man a machine, God made him a machine. I am merely calling attention to the fact, nothing more. Is it wrong to call attention to the fact? Is it a crime?

Y. M. I think it is wrong to *expose* a fact when harm can come of it.

O. M. Go on.

Y. M. Look at the matter as it stands now. Man has been taught that he is the supreme marvel of the Creation; he believes it; in all the ages he has never doubted it, whether he was a naked savage, or clothed in purple and fine linen, and civilized. This has made his heart buoyant, his life cheery. His pride in himself, his sincere admiration of himself, his joy in what he supposed were his own and unassisted achievements, and his exultation over the praise and applause which they evoked—these have exalted him, enthused him, ambitioned him to higher and higher flights; in a word, made his life worth the living. But by your scheme, all this is abolished; he is degraded to a machine, he is a nobody, his noble prides wither to mere vanities; let him strive as he may, he can never be any better than

his humblest and stupidest neighbor; he would never
be cheerful again, his life would not be worth the
living.

O. M. You really think that?

Y. M. I certainly do.

O. M. Have you ever seen me uncheerful, unhappy?

Y. M. No.

O. M. Well, *I* believe these things. Why have
they not made me unhappy?

Y. M. Oh, well—temperament, of course! You
never let *that* escape from your scheme.

O. M. That is correct. If a man is born with an
unhappy temperament, nothing can make him
happy; if he is born with a happy temperament,
nothing can make him unhappy.

Y. M. What—not even a degrading and heart-
chilling system of beliefs?

O. M. Beliefs? Mere beliefs? Mere convictions? They are powerless. They strive in vain
against inborn temperament.

Y. M. I can't believe that, and I don't.

O. M. Now you are speaking hastily. It shows
that you have not studiously examined the facts.
Of all your intimates, which one is the happiest?
Is n't it Burgess?

Y. M. Easily.

O. M. And which one is the unhappiest? Henry Adams?

Y. M. Without a question!

O. M. I know them well. They are extremes, abnormals; their temperaments are as opposite as the poles. Their life-histories are about alike—but look at the results! Their ages are about the same—around about fifty. Burgess has always been buoyant, hopeful, happy; Adams has always been cheerless, hopeless, despondent. As young fellows, both tried country journalism—and failed. Burgess did n't seem to mind it; Adams could n't smile, he could only mourn and groan over what had happened, and torture himself with vain regrets for not having done so-and-so instead of so-and-so—*then* he would have succeeded. They tried the law—and failed. Burgess remained happy—because he could n't help it, Adams was wretched—because he could n't help it. From that day to this, those two men have gone on trying things and failing: Burgess has come out happy and cheerful every time, Adams the reverse. And we do absolutely know that these men's inborn temperaments have remained unchanged through all the vicissitudes of their material affairs. Let us see how it is with their

immaterialities. Both have been zealous demo-
crats; both have been zealous republicans; both have
been zealous mugwumps. Burgess has always
found happiness and Adams unhappiness, in these
several political beliefs and in their migrations out
of them. Both of these men have been Presbyterians, Universalists, Methodists, Catholics—then
Presbyterians again, then Methodists again. Burgess has always found rest in these excursions, and
Adams unrest. They are trying Christian Science,
now, with the customary result, the inevitable result.
No political or religious belief can make Burgess
unhappy or the other man happy. I assure you
it is purely a matter of temperament. Beliefs
are *acquirements*, temperaments are *born;* beliefs
are subject to change, nothing whatever can change
temperament.

Y. M. You have instanced extreme temperaments.

O. M. Yes. The half-dozen others are modifica-
tions of the extremes. But the law is the same.
Where the temperament is two-thirds happy, or two-
thirds unhappy, no political or religious beliefs can
change the proportions. The vast majority of
temperaments are pretty equally balanced; the in-
tensities are absent, and this enables a nation to learn
to accomodate itself to its political and religious cir-

cumstances and like them, be satisfied with them, at last prefer them. Nations do not *think,* they only *feel.* They get their feelings at second-hand through their temperaments, not their brains. A nation can be brought—by force of circumstances, not argument—to reconcile itself to *any kind of government or religion that can be devised;* in time it will fit itself to the required conditions; later, it will prefer them; and will fiercely fight for them. As instances, you have all history: the Greeks, the Romans, the Persians, the Egyptians, the Russians, the Germans, the French, the English, the Spaniards, the Americans, the South Americans, the Japanese, the Chinese, the Hindoos, the Turks—a thousand wild and tame religions, every kind of government that can be thought of, from tiger to house-cat, each nation *knowing* it has the only true religion and the only sane system of government, each despising all the others, each an ass and not suspecting it, each proud of its fancied supremacy, each perfectly sure it is the pet of God, each with undoubting confidence summoning Him to take command in time of war, each surprised when He goes over to the enemy, but by habit able to excuse it and resume compliments—in a word, the whole human race content, always content, persistently content, indestructibly content, happy, thankful, proud, *no matter what its religion is, nor whether its master be tiger or house-cat.* Am I stating facts? You know I am. Is the human race cheerful? You know it is. Considering what it can stand, and be happy, you do me too much honor when you think that *I* can place before it a system of plain cold facts that can take the cheerfulness out of it. Nothing can do that. Everything has been tried. Without success. I beg you not to be troubled.

AFTERWORD

Linda Wagner-Martin

Is there a shying away from the products of a writer's old age, a reluctance to read them seriously? Do critics mistrust so-called changes as one voice or another begins to dominate later work, creating a persona that seems different — or at least at variance with — what has been considered "characteristic"? Perhaps the tendency to value early or mid-career work has prejudiced readers' reaction to Mark Twain's *What Is Man?* (1906).

By 1906, Mark Twain was a snowy-haired septuagenarian. He liked to claim that he had hated life since eighteen, but his fulminating about the baseness of human beings had become more noticeable as he aged. Always the performance artist, Twain may have exacerbated his family's distaste for his somber philosophizing; whenever he began to express his dour skepticism, Livy, his beloved wife, "would not even listen." In the words of his biographer Justin Kaplan, "Livy loathed [*What Is Man?*], shuddered over it."[1] For Twain, however, the mock Socratic dialogue was his "Bible," and entries from his notebook suggests that such ruminating was not atypical.

> All schools, all colleges, have two great functions: to confer, and to conceal valuable knowledge.

> Sixty years ago optimist and fool were not synonymous terms. This is a greater change than that wrought by science and invention.

> God is Might (and He is shifty, malicious, and uncertain).

> None but the dead are permitted to speak the truth.[2]

Livy was not the only one to dislike her husband's ideas. Mark Twain's sporadic intellectual despair was received coolly, if not with outright distaste, by his friends in Hartford's Monday Evening Club, an elite group limited to twenty men. A member since the early 1870s, he looked forward to the bi-weekly meetings, often inviting such out-of-town friends as William Dean Howells and E. C. Stedman to attend, promising them a "rattling good time." He relished exchanging ideas with Calvin Stowe, Charles Dudley Warner, Horace Bushnell, Nathaniel Burton, Edwin Parker, and others of scholarly or theological bent. On various occasions, Twain had presented papers on universal suffrage (he argued for the women's vote), on the stupidity of the press, on the weaknesses of the Republican party, and on the phenomenon of conscience ("The Facts Concerning the Recent Carnival of Crime in Connecticut"). But in 1881, when he read a paper titled *What Is Man?* to the club, he was surprised at the vehemence with which the members rejected it, calling it "a lie, a thousand times a lie!"[3]

The attention the author gave this short work continued. Two years later he tested the club members' reaction again, with an essay titled differently. "What Is Happiness?" was greeted in the same pessimistic spirit. If man is "an exteriorly determined machine, with no originality of idea and no freedom of will," and happiness is "exclusive satisfaction of one's own temperamental and spiritual needs,"[4] then — according to Twain — the enticements, and rewards, of both humanism and Christianity are meaningless.

Twain's mood seemed clear. By 1897, when he wrote to John Adams, the English psychologist, that *What Is Man?* was a book about psychology, he had already written, discussed, meditated upon, lamented, and self-consciously revised and reorganized the dialogue many times. He claimed with apparent accuracy in the preface to the 1906 edition, the work's first publication, that his studies for the essay were "begun twenty-five or twenty-seven years ago," and that he had gone over the text of *What Is Man?* many times in the past eight years.

Published anonymously by DeVinne Press in an edition of two hundred and fifty copies, the finished product was polished, showing little sign of Twain's many additions, deletions, and changes both large and small. Half of the present essay was written between April and July of 1898, in Vienna. Some parts (e.g., "The Quality of Man," his elaboration on considerations of God) were later cut; other segments were added. The 1898 version, known as "the Vienna typescript," was the basis for the second text, typed in 1902. It differs appreciably from the first, as does the third, of 1905. The work was distributed in August of 1906, copyrighted in the name of J. W. Bothwell, the superintendent of DeVinne, and accompanied by a letter signed by that gentleman. It attracted so little notice, however, that Twain later said he had erred in publishing it.

Perhaps the lack of attention was just as well. For in Twain's case, a text that has usually been read as an echo of Nietzsche, Ibsen, or Shaw, and criticized for its cynicism and bitterness, was more likely to shock his customary readers than to interest them. Mark Twain had made his reputation (and his fortunes) on his humorous writings and lectures. Blatant skepticism would scarcely have been admissible from the creator of Tom Sawyer, Huck Finn, Mississippi River pilots, and a few recalcitrant jumping frogs.

In literary history, Mark Twain's gently realistic depictions of "American" life had been truly originary; and if his readers chose to see his portraits of the citizens of his worlds as comic, he left them room to do so. (Most of his best drawings of character were multivalent, or at least ambivalent, and frequently indicted the society that was responsible for the many lost children, wayward adolescents, and runaways of all hues that peopled his narratives.) His work had influenced an entire school of writers who prized the vernacular, the truly "American idiom." And it had sanctioned a kind of romantic realism, in which happy (or at least satisfying) endings could exist side by side with some sense of social reality. Although Twain let Huck escape from Pap Finn's clutches in a junior version of the Yankee trickster legend that was more than a bit implausible, he did not blink at class difference: Huck's pap was an unfortunate fact of nineteenth-century American life.

But even if one might say that Mark Twain's reputation as a comfortably comic writer in his early and middle works existed as much in critics' minds as in his oeuvre, his shift to the sometimes bitter interchanges in *What Is Man?* would not have been easy for readers to accept. Those that knew of the work looked first at Mark Twain's life. And that life in the dozen years which preceded the strange narrative gave them plenty of reason to think their beloved author was writing out of his considerable personal pain.

By 1894 the substantial fortune Twain had amassed from his writing and speaking career had been eaten away through a series of unwise investments — chief among them was the Paige typesetter, fascinating to Twain for what he considered its technological sophistication. Bankruptcy brought him back to reality with a jolt: if he was not responsible for the lives of his wife and daughters, not to mention his own, no one else would assume that task. Attempting to salvage what he could, he took on an arduous worldwide speaking tour.

Twain's finances were extremely unpredictable. On occasion, he made more money than planned. But on the tour that began in 1895, when he, Livy, and their daughter Clara sailed for Australia, his profit was much less than anticipated: some lectures were canceled, expenses were high, and the entire trip was exhausting. And the tragedy of the long absence was not merely financial. In the parents' year abroad, their daughters Jean and Susy remained in the States, and Susy, the difficult and talented child, contracted meningitis. By the time the Clemenses were notified of her illness, in the summer of 1896, she was beyond saving. Even though Livy and Clara sailed immediately from England, Susy died before they reached the States.

Clearly, in the lives of both her parents, Susy's death was not only the tragedy of their existence; it was also an indication of their guilt as parents. Their private writings suggest that they believed she would not have died if they had been with her. Mark Twain's guilt was immense: not only was he unable to save his much-loved Susy's life; he also missed her burial. And it had been his foolhardy investments that led to the bankruptcy in the first place. His guilt, like his grief, was ineradicable.

According to Sherwood Cummings, so driven did Twain become that observers might have noticed little change in the author's behavior. After Susy's death, he wrote "as voluminously as before," but now most of his writing was private, and it was dominated by three ideas: "the uncaringness of god, the law of one's nature, and the dual personality."[5] The kinds of questions that had so dismayed the Monday Evening Club now took on a terrible urgency as Twain groped for some reason, some explanation, for the death of his innocent child.

Obsessive in his torment, Twain confirmed Livy in her own grief— neither saw any relief from the guilty mourning that marked their lives. (By 1898, having paid off most of his earlier debts, Twain was making more bad investments, this time in a high-protein food concentrate, only adding to the worries of his good helpmeet: Livy kept the financial records for the household.) By the summer of 1902, Livy was plagued with symptoms of what would become her last illness — asthma, nervous prostration, hyperthyroid heart disease. She died in Italy on June 5, 1904, after twenty-two months of invalidism, months during which Twain was allowed to see her only once a day and sometimes not at all. Following Livy's death, their daughter Jean had a major epileptic seizure and was institutionalized frequently during the five years that remained to her; and Clara began the pattern of breakdown that would often isolate her (during her hospitalization in 1904-5, for instance, Twain was not permitted to see her at all, nor even to telephone her).

No human being would have been unmarked by such tragedies, but to attribute Twain's sentiments in *What Is Man?* entirely to biography is to simplify. From the point of view of continuity in the author's literary production, in the life of his own writing, the troubling essay can be seen as a culmination of the strains of interrogation of both social and religious systems that run through much of his work. In fact, one can read Twain's fiction backward from the perspective of the issues that surface in *What Is Man?* and discern a consistency that the sage of Hartford would have found unsurprising. To the question of the title, Twain had earlier provided inescapably bleak answers in narratives as varied as "The Story of the Bad Little Boy Who Didn't Come to Grief," "Cannibalism in the Cars," "The Curious Republic of Gondour," *Pudd'nhead Wilson*, and, most visibly, *A Connecticut Yankee in King Arthur's Court*.

Read moralistically, much of Twain's writing suggests that men exist to cheat their fellow human beings, and even if that cheating is somehow disguised (in this nineteenth-century era of valorizing the con man), someone has been bested. The author's pessimism was even more apparent in the *Mysterious Stranger* stories, written between 1897 and 1908, and "The Man That Corrupted Hadleyburg" (1899).

Twain's dialogue in *What Is Man?* can also be read as Bakhtinian. Because the author was seventy at the time of publication, readers have tended to equate him with the Old Man. To make such an equation is to privilege the Old Man's sentiments. It might be suggested that the dialogue form was a literary choice rather than a biographical one: he expressed his ideas in a format conventional in philosophic, religious, or humanistic discourse. The conventions of the dialogue, after all, lead readers to value *each* speaker; each voice expresses concepts, and it is the dialogic interplay that brings home the meaning of the interrogation. If there were not some inherent value in each part, the author might as well write a straightforward essay, something on the model of Ralph Waldo Emerson's "The Poet" or "The American Scholar." Instead, Twain's implicit models were surely the popular "conversations" so important in the intellectual circles comprised of his peers, especially after he moved to Hartford.

Twain's choice was the dialogue; and in presenting each side of the interchange, he forces the reader to have sympathy for both the young speaker, who wants to believe in an ideationally positive, human-centered world, and the old, even though the latter poses as a weary cynic, or at least as a man who has been forced to accept the fashionable doctrines of mechanistic determinism. The dialogue between Young Man and Old Man represents Twain's fascination with twins, or with the psychological state of divided consciousness. Of Twain's "two" characters in the essay, the young wants to focus on the good in humankind; the old, on the evil — albeit an unwitting evil, less malicious than mechanistic. Conjoining these personae, finding a midpoint, the reader can see the unity between the two, the bond of twinship. A problematic question, unasked in the text, then becomes, Where on that continuum between good and evil does the human heart really lie?

Read in a less abstract way, Young Man and Old Man represent Twain as the aging Samuel Clemens, looking back into his several belief systems and wondering from his vantage point of maturity at his earlier naive acceptance of Christian teachings. That naiveté is the core of the Young Man character. A section of the text called "A Little Story" suggests a further realization, however: that the Christian belief system is as good as any; and that the supposedly intellectually superior Infidel who deprives a dying boy of its comfort has done irretrievable damage. (Biography enters here again, because Twain had stripped Livy's deep religious faith early in their marriage; and one of his sorrows at her death was her inability to believe in any future existence.) To clarify his point, the Old Man goes on with the story; ironically, when the Infidel himself becomes a Christian and goes to a pagan country as a missionary, he again leads a dying boy away from his beliefs, only to find him, too, in despair at the time of his death. The value of belief, Twain's dialogue makes clear, lies not in content but in the ability to accept a belief — any belief.

The dialogue also expresses a simple reality: aging does bifurcate the human consciousness, because one continues to feel "young"; at sixty or seventy we remain the same to ourselves as forty or fifty years before. Yet in the eyes of the observing world — eyes Twain was thoroughly conscious of throughout his career — one grows "old." The author's dramatic use of costume and his sense of style suggest his wanting to remain indomitably young (and whimsical and unpredictable — and therefore, perhaps, likable) even as he ineluctably aged.

As a composite of seven parts, *What Is Man?* intentionally repeats key ideas. The headings for some of the sections indicate the philosophic direction of the argument: "Man the Machine," "Personal Merit," "Man's Sole Impulse — The Securing of His Own Approval," "Training," "Instinct and Thought," "Free Will," "The Master-Passion." Scattered through the dialogue are set pieces of illustration, titled descriptively: "A Little Story," "A Parable," "Further Instances." As the two protagonists debate, circling back to their premier arguments, the work moves like a narrative — and it was probably this rhythm Twain was striving for as he added, rearranged, and deleted.

The most startling opinion in the first part is the Old Man's contention that man is a machine, an organism totally without free will. Continual repetition works to reinforce this claim, and the repetition seems necessary to pierce the Young Man's obdurate resistance. Simplistic in its firm reiteration, the Old Man's argument never tackles the central issue — whether or not God exists — but instead begins at the human end of the continuum, assessing the obvious imperfectibility of the human race. Given only to self-gratification, an individual may commit brave acts or self-sacrificing ones, the Old Man says, but he does so solely because his own nature is pleased by such acts. Calling this the "Master Impulse," the Old Man remains confident of his assessment, which he elaborates in some detail in parts 2 and 3 while the Young Man worries, questions, and finally attacks him for this "Gospel of Self-Approval."

Part 4 focuses on "training," which the Old Man defines as any outside influence, cultural as well as educational. Every person is the product of a complex of forces, a "chameleon" who "by the law of his nature . . . takes the color of his place of resort." After examples of the powerlessness of the human mind to avoid being so trained, the dialogue returns in parts 5 and 6 to the initial contention, that man is a machine, incapable of creating, formed only to respond. The Old Man describes human thought as a mechanistic process — observing, inferring, adding, concluding. Apart from this reductive activity, "thinking" or "reasoning" cannot exist. The notion of free will is suspect because the mind, trained to respond as it has been, cannot upset mechanical patterns to make unexpected choices: even personal life choices are the result of training. Therefore, free will is nothing more than a misnomer.

Here the Young Man attacks, charging the Old Man with "elusive terminology." From this pivotal point they resume discussion of the "Master-Passion," the conscience, defined as merely another manifestation of "the hunger for Self-Approval" as determined by the various temperaments. When the Young Man questions the dominance of temperament in this "degrading and heart-chilling system of beliefs," the Old Man assures him that the philosophical undertaking they have just been engaged in has had, in fact, little effect on either of their inherited temperaments. The Old Man repeats that man is not superior to animals; in fact, because animals never knowingly do evil, they are probably superior to men. Neither is the mind more spiritual or moral than the body. And while the Old Man accepts a kind of limited faculty he calls "free choice," he declares again that free will does not exist.

As the dialogue concludes, the Old Man assumes that he has won (the discussion has become so intense that the Young Man has taken a holiday), and spends the last few paragraphs consoling his interlocutor. The Old Man points out that although he has adopted this belief system, which itself is dehumanizing and cheerless, he remains cheerful. When the Young Man argues that such an attitude is the result of temperament, the Old Man replies, "If a man is born with an unhappy temperament, nothing can make him happy; if he is born with a happy temperament, nothing can make him unhappy." Solipsism seems to be one of the terms of the ongoing discussion.

The dialogue ends with the Old Man admonishing the Young Man "not to be troubled." Whether his assurance is sophistry or compassion, or a simple move toward conclusion, Twain does not indicate.

When Twain died in 1910, the *New York Tribune* published a feature article about *What Is Man?* Most of the commentary focused on the incongruity that the greatest of America's humorists had had such dark, and in some views antireligious, sentiments. Subsequent critics, however, have tended to see the work as an integral part of the author's late prose. I am proposing that we see it as a more integral part of all his prose, as a thread that runs through even the lightest of his fiction, the calmest of his memoirs; and as the questioning hook that may provide a rationale for his becoming a writer in the first place. It was clear to Mark Twain that he could not accept the sanctimonious platitudes that some nineteenth-century Americans pretended to believe. It was also clear that a number of other citizens of the world shared his innate skepticism about knowledge, religious belief, and man's duty to his peers. More often than not, Twain made his fortune writing about people who themselves questioned the verities which society tried to repackage as general truth.

Mark Twain also subverted the literary language he saw as conniving to provide only pap to readers; and he did it, naturally, by creating a new language — or at least one different enough that it could call into question some of the locutions and patterns that constituted basic polite discourse. In most guises, this new language made use of dialect and dialogue that captured local color — spelling words as they would have been pronounced, using comparatively impolite expressions to suit particular characters — so that readers responded to what appeared to be idiomatically vivid speech without realizing consciously that Twain's meaning went beyond what they expected.

His use of conventional locutions and diction in *What Is Man?*, however, erased all prior disguise: here was Mark Twain saying things that many readers did not want to hear, introducing topics they did not want to discuss, and prodding them (rather than entertaining them) to question their deepest principles. The dialogue was not meant to be fun. Or funny. Or a mere pastime. It was intended to be what it was, a fairly rigorous philosophical exercise. Once more, Mark Twain's brilliance as a writer overtook whatever purpose he thought he was serving in his text, and brought home to readers the insistently complex and always intricate path of coming to understanding. In his own attempts at creating an epistemology that might explain loss and disappointment, Mark Twain turned to writing. And the sometimes enigmatic *What Is Man?* remains as one testament to his ability to grapple with ideas that the polite society of the "successful" would rather suppress.

NOTES

1. Justin Kaplan, *Mr. Clemens and Mark Twain* (New York: Simon and Schuster, 1966), 337–40.

2. *Mark Twain's Notebook*, ed. Albert Bigelow Paine (New York: Harper and Brothers, 1935), 393–95.

3. Kenneth R. Andrews, *Nook Farm: Mark Twain's Hartford Circle* (Cambridge: Harvard University Press, 1950), 103.

4. Frank Baldanza, *Mark Twain: An Introduction and Interpretation* (Totowa, N.J.: Barnes and Noble, 1961), 133.

5. Sherwood Cummings, *Mark Twain and Science: Adventures of a Mind* (Baton Rouge: Louisiana State University Press, 1988), 202.

FOR FURTHER READING

Linda Wagner-Martin

The standard biographies of Twain are Justin Kaplan's *Mr. Clemens and Mark Twain* (New York: Simon and Schuster, 1966), Louis J. Budd's *Our Mark Twain: The Making of His Public Personality* (Philadelphia: University of Pennsylvania Press, 1983), and Everett Emerson's *The Authentic Mark Twain* (Philadelphia: University of Pennsylvania Press, 1984). New kinds of perceptions about the author's life are available in Susan Gillman's *Dark Twins: Imposture and Identity in Mark Twain's America* (Chicago: University of Chicago Press, 1989), Richard Bridgman's *Traveling in Mark Twain* (Berkeley: University of California Press, 1987), Peter Stoneley's *Mark Twain and the Feminine Aesthetic* (New York: Cambridge University Press, 1992), Laura E. Skandera-Trombley's *Mark Twain in the Company of Women* (Philadelphia: University of Pennsylvania Press, 1994), and Shelley Fisher Fishkin's *Was Huck Black? Mark Twain and African-American Voices* (New York: Oxford University Press, 1993).

Relevant readings of *What Is Man?* and of this period of Twain's career can be found in Kenneth R. Andrews' *Nook Farm: Mark Twain's Hartford Circle* (Cambridge: Harvard University Press, 1950), William R. Macnaughton's *Mark Twain's Last Years as a Writer* (Columbia: University of Missouri Press, 1979), Frank Baldanza's *Mark Twain: An Introduction and Interpretation* (Totowa, N.J.: Barnes and Noble, 1961), Susan K. Harris's *Mark Twain's Escape from Time: A Study of Patterns and Images* (Columbia: University of Missouri Press, 1982), James D. Hart's "*What Is Man?*" in *The Oxford Companion to American Literature* (1983 edition); Paul Baender's introduction to *What Is Man? and Other Philosophical Writings* (Berkeley: University of California Press, 1973), pp. 1–34, and Sherwood Cummings' *Mark Twain and Science: Adventures of a Mind* (Baton Rouge: Louisiana State University Press, 1988). Of special use in this essay were *Mark Twain's Notebook*, ed. Albert Bigelow Paine (New York: Harper and Brothers, 1935), and John S. Tuckey's "Mark Twain's Later Dialogue: The 'Me' and the Machine," *American Literature* 41 (1970): 532–42.

A NOTE ON THE TEXT

Robert H. Hirst

This text of *What Is Man?* is a photographic facsimile of a copy of the first American edition, all known copies of which are dated 1906 on the title page. That edition was limited to 250 copies, published privately in August 1906; two copies were deposited with the Copyright Office on August 20. The copy reproduced here is an example of Jacob Blanck's "second issue," in which the leaf containing page 131 is a cancel and the last words on that page are corrected to 'thinks about it.' rather than 'thinks about' (*BAL* 3490). This copy is numbered 240. It is in the collection of the Mark Twain House in Hartford, Connecticut (810/C625wha/1906).

THE MARK TWAIN HOUSE

The Mark Twain House is a museum and research center dedicated to the study of Mark Twain, his works, and his times. The museum is located in the nineteen-room mansion in Hartford, Connecticut, built for and lived in by Samuel L. Clemens, his wife, and their three children, from 1874 to 1891. The Picturesque Gothic-style residence, with interior design by the firm of Louis Comfort Tiffany and Associated Artists, is one of the premier examples of domestic Victorian architecture in America. Clemens wrote *Adventures of Huckleberry Finn*, *The Adventures of Tom Sawyer*, *A Connecticut Yankee in King Arthur's Court*, *The Prince and the Pauper*, and *Life on the Mississippi* while living in Hartford.

The Mark Twain House is open year-round. In addition to tours of the house, the educational programs of the Mark Twain House include symposia, lectures, and teacher training seminars that focus on the contemporary relevance of Twain's legacy. Past programs have featured discussions of literary censorship with playwright Arthur Miller and writer William Styron; of the power of language with journalist Clarence Page, comedian Dick Gregory, and writer Gloria Naylor; and of the challenges of teaching *Adventures of Huckleberry Finn* amidst charges of racism.

CONTRIBUTORS

Shelley Fisher Fishkin, professor of American Studies and English at the University of Texas at Austin, is the author of the award-winning books *Was Huck Black? Mark Twain and African-American Voices* (1993) and *From Fact to Fiction: Journalism and Imaginative Writing in America* (1985). Her most recent book is *Lighting Out for the Territory: Reflections on Mark Twain and American Culture* (1996). She holds a Ph.D. in American Studies from Yale University, has lectured on Mark Twain in Belgium, England, France, Israel, Italy, Mexico, the Netherlands, and Turkey, as well as throughout the United States, and is president-elect of the Mark Twain Circle of America.

Robert H. Hirst is the General Editor of the Mark Twain Project at The Bancroft Library, University of California in Berkeley. Apart from that, he has no other known eccentricities.

Charles Johnson is the author of *Middle Passage*, which won the 1990 National Book Award for Fiction, of the novels *Faith and the Good Thing* (1974) and *Oxherding Tale* (1982), and of a story collection, *The Sorcerer's Apprentice* (1986), a work of aesthetics, *Being and Race: Black Writing Since 1970* (1988), two collections of drawings, and more than twenty screenplays. He is completing a new novel, *Dreamer*, and co-editing an anthology on black males in America, forthcoming from Indiana University Press. Professor of English at the University of Washington, where he holds an endowed chair, the Pollock Professorship for Excellence in English, he lives in Seattle.

Linda Wagner-Martin is Hanes Professor of English and Comparative Literature at the University of North Carolina at Chapel Hill. Recipient of grants from the National Endowment of the Humanities and the Guggenheim and Rockefeller Foundations, she has published widely on American literature. Recent books include an edition of John Steinbeck's *The Pearl* (1994), an anatomy of women's biography titled *Telling Women's*

Lives: The New Biography (1994), *"Favored Strangers": Gertrude Stein and Her Family* (1995), and *New Essays on Faulkner's Go Down, Moses* (1996). She also co-edited *The Oxford Companion to Women's Writing in the United States* (1995) and its accompanying anthology, *The Oxford Book of Women's Writing in the United States* (1995).

ACKNOWLEDGMENTS

There are a number of people without whom The Oxford Mark Twain would not have happened. I am indebted to Laura Brown, senior vice president and trade publisher, Oxford University Press, for suggesting that I edit an "Oxford Mark Twain," and for being so enthusiastic when I proposed that it take the present form. Her guidance and vision have informed the entire undertaking.

Crucial as well, from the earliest to the final stages, was the help of John Boyer, executive director of the Mark Twain House, who recognized the importance of the project and gave it his wholehearted support.

My father, Milton Fisher, believed in this project from the start and helped nurture it every step of the way, as did my stepmother, Carol Plaine Fisher. Their encouragement and support made it all possible. The memory of my mother, Renée B. Fisher, sustained me throughout.

I am enormously grateful to all the contributors to The Oxford Mark Twain for the effort they put into their essays, and for having been such fine, collegial collaborators. Each came through, just as I'd hoped, with fresh insights and lively prose. It was a privilege and a pleasure to work with them, and I value the friendships that we forged in the process.

In addition to writing his fine afterword, Louis J. Budd provided invaluable advice and support, even going so far as to read each of the essays for accuracy. All of us involved in this project are greatly in his debt. Both his knowledge of Mark Twain's work and his generosity as a colleague are legendary and unsurpassed.

Elizabeth Maguire's commitment to The Oxford Mark Twain during her time as senior editor at Oxford was exemplary. When the project proved to be more ambitious and complicated than any of us had expected, Liz helped make it not only manageable, but fun. Assistant editor Elda Rotor's wonderful help in coordinating all aspects of The Oxford Mark Twain, along with literature editor T. Susan Chang's enthusiastic involvement with the project in its final stages, helped bring it all to fruition.

I am extremely grateful to Joy Johannessen for her astute and sensitive copyediting, and for having been such a pleasure to work with. And I appreciate the conscientiousness and good humor with which Kathy Kuhtz Campbell heroically supervised all aspects of the set's production. Oxford president Edward Barry, vice president and editorial director Helen McInnis, marketing director Amy Roberts, publicity director Susan Rotermund, art director David Tran, trade editorial, design and production manager Adam Bohannon, trade advertising and promotion manager Woody Gilmartin, director of manufacturing Benjamin Lee, and the entire staff at Oxford were as supportive a team as any editor could desire.

The staff of the Mark Twain House provided superb assistance as well. I would like to thank Marianne Curling, curator, Debra Petke, education director, Beverly Zell, curator of photography, Britt Gustafson, assistant director of education, Beth Ann McPherson, assistant curator, and Pam Collins, administrative assistant, for all their generous help, and for allowing us to reproduce books and photographs from the Mark Twain House collection. One could not ask for more congenial or helpful partners in publishing.

G. Thomas Tanselle, vice president of the John Simon Guggenheim Memorial Foundation, and an expert on the history of the book, offered essential advice about how to create as responsible a facsimile edition as possible. I appreciate his very knowledgeable counsel.

I am deeply indebted to Robert H. Hirst, general editor of the Mark Twain Project at The Bancroft Library in Berkeley, for bringing his outstanding knowledge of Twain editions to bear on the selection of the books photographed for the facsimiles, for giving generous assistance all along the way, and for providing his meticulous notes on the text. The set is the richer for his advice. I would also like to express my gratitude to the Mark Twain Project, not only for making texts and photographs from their collection available to us, but also for nurturing Mark Twain studies with a steady infusion of matchless, important publications.

I would like to thank Jeffrey Kaimowitz, curator of the Watkinson Library at Trinity College, Hartford (where the Mark Twain House collection is kept), along with his colleagues Peter Knapp and Alesandra M. Schmidt, for having been instrumental in Robert Hirst's search for first editions that could be safely reproduced. Victor Fischer, Harriet Elinor Smith, and especially Kenneth M. Sanderson, associate editors with the Mark Twain Project, reviewed the note on the text in each volume with cheerful vigilance. Thanks are also due to Mark Twain Project associate editor Michael Frank and administrative assistant Brenda J. Bailey for their help at various stages.

I am grateful to Helen K. Copley for granting permission to publish photographs in the Mark Twain Collection of the James S. Copley Library in La Jolla, California, and to Carol Beales and Ron Vanderhye of the Copley Library for making my research trip to their institution so productive and enjoyable.

Several contributors — David Bradley, Louis J. Budd, Beverly R. David, Robert Hirst, Fred Kaplan, James S. Leonard, Toni Morrison, Lillian S. Robinson, Jeffrey Rubin-Dorsky, Ray Sapirstein, and David L. Smith — were particularly helpful in the early stages of the project, brainstorming about the cast of writers and scholars who could make it work. Others who participated in that process were John Boyer, James Cox, Robert Crunden, Joel Dinerstein, William Goetzmann, Calvin and Maria Johnson, Jim Magnuson, Arnold Rampersad, Siva Vaidhyanathan, Steve and Louise Weinberg, and Richard Yarborough.

Kevin Bochynski, famous among Twain scholars as an "angel" who is gifted at finding methods of making their research run more smoothly, was helpful in more ways than I can count. He did an outstanding job in his official capacity as production consultant to The Oxford Mark Twain, supervising the photography of the facsimiles. I am also grateful to him for having put me in touch via e-mail with Kent Rasmussen, author of the magisterial *Mark Twain A to Z*, who was tremendously helpful as the project proceeded, sharing insights on obscure illustrators and other points, and generously being "on call" for all sorts of unforeseen contingencies.

I am indebted to Siva Vaidhyanathan of the American Studies Program of the University of Texas at Austin for having been such a superb research assistant. It would be hard to imagine The Oxford Mark Twain without the benefit of his insights and energy. A fine scholar and writer in his own right, he was crucial to making this project happen.

Georgia Barnhill, the Andrew W. Mellon Curator of Graphic Arts at the American Antiquarian Society in Worcester, Massachusetts, Tom Staley, director of the Harry Ransom Humanities Research Center at the University of Texas at Austin, and Joan Grant, director of collection services at the Elmer Holmes Bobst Library of New York University, granted us access to their collections and assisted us in the reproduction of several volumes of The Oxford Mark Twain. I would also like to thank Kenneth Craven, Sally Leach, and Richard Oram of the Harry Ransom Humanities Research Center for their help in making HRC materials available, and Jay and John Crowley, of Jay's Publishers Services in Rockland, Massachusetts, for their efforts to photograph the books carefully and attentively.

I would like to express my gratitude for the grant I was awarded by the University Research Institute of the University of Texas at Austin to defray some of the costs of researching The Oxford Mark Twain. I am also grateful to American Studies director Robert Abzug and the University of Texas for the computer that facilitated my work on this project (and to UT systems analyst Steve Alemán, who tried his best to repair the damage when it crashed). Thanks also to American Studies administrative assistant Janice Bradley and graduate coordinator Melanie Livingston for their always generous and thoughtful help.

The Oxford Mark Twain would not have happened without the unstinting, wholehearted support of my husband, Jim Fishkin, who went way beyond the proverbial call of duty more times than I'm sure he cares to remember as he shared me unselfishly with that other man in my life, Mark Twain. I am also grateful to my family — to my sons Joey and Bobby, who cheered me on all along the way, as did Fannie Fishkin, David Fishkin, Gennie Gordon, Mildred Hope Witkin, and Leonard, Gillis, and Moss

Plaine — and to honorary family member Margaret Osborne, who did the same.

My greatest debt is to the man who set all this in motion. Only a figure as rich and complicated as Mark Twain could have sustained such energy and interest on the part of so many people for so long. Never boring, never dull, Mark Twain repays our attention again and again and again. It is a privilege to be able to honor his memory with The Oxford Mark Twain.

Shelley Fisher Fishkin
Austin, Texas
April 1996